Who are God's Guerrillas?

Who are God's Guerrillas?

Stuart Gramenz

Sovereign World

Sovereign World Ltd.
P.O. Box 17
Chichester PO20 6RY
England

Sovereign World Edition 1988

Unless otherwise stated all Scripture quotations are from the New King James Bible © 1984 Thomas Nelson Inc., Nashville, U.S.A.

Encyclopaedia quotations are taken from the 15th edition of the Encyclopaedia Brittanica printed in 1985 in the U.S.A., Volume 29, pages 681, 684, 686.

Cartoons by Kevin Rankin.

ISBN 1 85240 020 X

Contents

Who Are God's Guerrillas?

GUERRILLAS – SURELY NOT?

The majority of Christians are well aware that a spiritual war is presently being fought, however, many have pictured it in terms of a conventional army.

Songs sung like "God's got an army marching through the land..." has conjured up in the minds of many a gigantic force of thousands sweeping across their country in one great move!

The "conventional army" thinking has hindered what God is initiating in the church today.

But "Guerrilas," you may say, "surely not"!

Today many guerrilla forces around the world have built a reputation as some iniquitous, disorganized rabble using hideous tactics.

Remember, satan is a counterfeiter and when he tries to copy something it ends up perverted.

Many guerrilla forces today are a result of that perversion.

We must not forget that if there is a perverted copy, somewhere there must be a perfect original.

God's Guerrillas are the original. Jesus did not send out a conventional, uniformed, army. He did not send thousands of soldiers all in line as one great force. He sent a non-uniformed, unconventional guerrilla style army working in small combat units.

This original guerrilla force standing for righteousness, used their weapons of preaching and healing to turn the world upside down.

He is wanting us to see the truths and principles used by the original forces. He is restoring these keys to the church today because He wants the world turned upside down again and the gospel preached to every creature.

To do this, He is raising a new order of soldiers like the early church, who will be a holy powerful army but unlike the conventional army we all tend to picture.

This book goes to great lengths to show who the present day Guerrillas are, how they are being trained, their present day targets and their results so far.

It will open the eyes of many and raise a new vision and hope within those who wish to see Jesus rule over all.

Chapter 1

THE ORIGINAL GUERRILLAS

When we think of 'GOD'S ARMY', 'GUERRILLAS' is not usually the immediate picture that comes to mind. Armies usually conjure up thoughts of thousands of men parading down the streets in smart uniforms, marching off to battle to the accompaniment of brass bands.

In the context of the Bible, we see Joshua and his mighty men all in battle array, armed as a gigantic Godly force, taking city after city in the promised land. This is the traditional kind of picture we tend to draw when thinking of ARMIES OF GOD.

God, of course, has an army today. However, there are many differences between God's Army of the old testament and His new testament force! The type of army Jesus dispatched was unlike any army ever seen before. They were not sent out as one gigantic army like Joshua's in full battle array, but as an unconventional guerrilla army.

"Guerrilla!" You might say "Surely not!"

Before we turn away in horror, we must understand what this type of warfare actually is. It is clearly described by the Encyclopaedia Britannica: *"Guerrilla warfare is a type of warfare characterized by irregular forces fighting small-scale limited actions, generally in conjunction with a larger political-military strategy, against orthodox military forces."*

Our Commander, Jesus Christ, has a global strategy to extend His rulership over the entire earth. To achieve this goal, He didn't send out one gigantic army of tens of thousands; He sent His small forces out "two by two" to win this kingdom little by little in smaller scale actions.

Britannica goes on to say: *"Guerrillas are usually nondescript in dress, unconventional in weapons and equipment, lack formal supply lines, and employ highly unorthodox tactics."*

God's original Guerrillas were not uniformed and were given extremely unconventional weapons and equipment to take this kingdom. They were simply given an order: *"And as you go, preach, saying, 'The kingdom of heaven is at hand. Heal the sick, cleanse the lepers, raise the dead, cast out demons. Freely you have received, freely give.'"* (Matthew 10:7-8)

Their supply lines certainly were purely reliant on the promise that their God would supply all their needs. These men certainly filled the qualifications of a guerrilla.

The main reason I believe we have difficulty in seeing God's soldiers as guerrillas lies in the image that modern day guerrilla forces have.

Today's guerrillas are pictured by many as some disorganized, evil rabble using iniquitous and hideous tactics.

Remember the father of all evil, the devil, is a counterfeiter. The trouble is when he tries to duplicate something, it always ends up perverted, and many of today's guerrillas and their tactics are an example of that perversion.

What we must not forget is that if they and their works are a perverted copy, somewhere there is a perfect original.

God's Guerrillas are that original. Perfectly exemplified by Jesus and His works and then by His disciples as they duplicated His tactics.

LAWFULLY RECOGNIZED

Even today, however, under the rules of war, guerrilla forces can be recognized, if they comply with certain standards. Encyclopaedia Britannica again instructs us: *"The Brussels International Conference of 1874 provided that, in order to be recognized as lawful belligerents, guerrillas must answer to a specific commander, wear a distinctive badge, carry arms openly, and conform in operations to the laws and customs of war. The Hague Conference on the rules of land warfare in 1899 and 1907 adopted this definition with a few modifications, and it is also contained in the Geneva Conventions (1949) on the laws of war."*

The standard of God's Guerrillas is unparalleled.

They did not skulk around hiding behind bushes, but proudly and publicly answered to their Commander, Jesus Christ, and conspicuously wore their badge of authority in His name.

They did not sneak around planting bombs under people,but broadcast that they were soldiers of the light. They openly carried the weapons of their warfare, preaching the gospel, casting out demons and laying hands on the sick.

Further, we will see that the Guerrilla principles used in this book are based on proven warfare tactics used by Moses, Joshua, Jehoshaphat, Nehemiah and Joel and their old testament forces.

God's Guerrillas were no secret, subversive counterfeit group, but an answer to the world's problems, blatantly sharing and demonstrating how life under their leader could be.

With their additional high ethical standards, they over-qualify on the prerequisites laid down in the Geneva Convention, and are unsurpassed by any worldly army. We need to see the meaning of guerrilla from its original Godly perspective and see that the new testament army should be proud to be recognized as ....

GOD'S GUERRILLAS.

Chapter 2

TODAY'S GUERRILLAS

Quite a few years ago my phone rang and I answered the call of a good friend of mine. He was the owner of a large and successful auto auction business, and at that time, he had only just come into the knowledge of the Holy Spirit. He told me how he had been witnessing to his staff, inviting them to his church and encouraging them. He had done everything he could but with no break-through. No one would go to services. "I've been reading your magazines on your crusades in India", he said. "The sick are healed and the unsaved see the reality of Jesus and then they accept Him." I nodded in agreement.

"I want you to do the same down here. Come down to the auction, pray for the sick and then they'll get saved." He paused for a moment and then queried, "That's right isn't it?"

I was a little taken back.

Now certainly we had seen great things in India in direct confrontational type of preaching and healing, but of course now we are talking about tough, no nonsense, no religion, Australians.

"That's what the Bible says," I answered protectively.

"Great," he said, "when can you come down?"

We subsequently arranged a lunch time meeting.

On the morning of the meeting, I had one of those challenging times in the office. Phone calls, unexpected visitors, which all pulled me way behind schedule. I raced across to the meeting with no preparation or thought to what I would say or do.

On entering his office I was faced with about 25 people of all different backgrounds. There were mechanics, office workers, janitors, salesmen all standing around waiting for me "to do some miracles".

The atmosphere was so cold I felt as though I had walked into a spiritual refrigerator. It was a straightforward encounter.

There was no intercessory prayer group praying in the next room, breaking down the powers of darkness.

There were no musicians bringing a peaceful and quiet atmosphere into the place.

There was just me and the refrigerator!

I realised they did not want some long winded preacher, and Paul did say to be all things to all men.

I stood up, took a deep breath, and said: "When the miracles start happening here today, it's not to make myself out as some big shot; it's to show you that Jesus Christ is real and is alive.!"

If nothing else, I had certainly gained their attention. I gave them a short gospel message and then began praying for different needs.

I guess there were around 20 different complaints healed in the short time of ministry.

Based on the evidence of the healing and the demonstration that Jesus Christ was indeed alive, I asked for commitment for forgiveness of sin and acceptance of Him as Lord.

As a result, five immediately responded and another two committed themselves later.

At first I was so disappointed, I thought after beginning to preach that all would make decisions. The Lord rebuked me very strongly and said: "How many churches are getting seven saved on Sunday?" "Here you are in an auto auction in their lunch hour!"

I said: "Sorry Lord, You did a great job!"

The Lord went on to show me why He had taken me to this place. Even though there were seven initial responses, the rest had witnessed the demonstration of His power. It was not a report on television. It was not a write-up in the newspaper. It was not at church where the person three rows over had been healed. It was their friends and fellow workers. They could see it was true.

Although the others did not make a decision, a seed of His reality was planted in their hearts. He went on and reminded me that not one of these people would go to church.

I said: "That's right Lord, my friend did everything short of breaking their arms to get them to come along to services. They would not go!"

"Realise," the Lord said, "that is the state of the majority of the people in this country. They do not wish to, and will not go to the churches."

"IF THE PEOPLE WILL NOT GO TO CHURCH,
THE CHURCH MUST GO TO THE PEOPLE!"

The Lord went on to say: "I brought you to this place to show what My army is to do. People will walk into offices, or wherever they work, into supermarkets, or at social engagements and be able to boldly proclaim the gospel and see signs and wonders following to confirm their word."

TODAY'S GUERRILLAS

A revival has already started and will continue to grow among many of those presently just warming church pews. They are going to rise up as His army and move out and touch the unsaved in their daily walks. I realised that this modern army would be like God's original guerrilla army.

Guerrilla means "little war".

This army would go around causing "little wars" wherever it went. Further study through encyclopaedias enabled me to come up with this composite definition:

"Guerrilla warfare is waged by roving bands of fighters who will torment and defeat the enemy with ambushes, sudden raids and full scale attacks. These bands usually operate behind enemy lines."

Doesn't this describe what happened at the auto auction? We did not entice the people into our ground, the church, but we took a sudden raid into their territory, defeating the enemy and set people free. This is how Jesus operated with His Guerrillas. They did not try to muster all the sinners into the synagogue—they went into enemy territory starting "little wars", using their weapons of preaching and healing.

My composite description goes on to say: *"Many guerrillas are civilians, not uniformed and are nondescript in dress. They work as farmers and labourers but act as guerrillas as well."*

God realizes that full time ministers with the uniforms of the cloth can make the enemy head for the hills when confronted. The secretaries, housewives, labourers, accountants—all Christians—are meeting targets every day. Not being in a uniform gives them the opportunity to get right alongside people and use the spiritual weapons of our warfare without causing alarm.

CHAPTER 3

YOU ARE AT WAR

Many saints today have not realized their active role in today's forces, and have some mystical type of idea that they can just sit back and watch, while God does all the work.

I am sure Joshua's old testament army had these same initial thoughts when God spoke these words to them before they were to enter the promised land.

"The Lord your God Himself crosses over before you; He will destroy these nations from before you, and you shall dispossess them" (Deuteromomy 31:3)

I am sure after hearing that, the early army got excited. "Wow! God's going to do it all; we just have to sit back and collect the spoils. What a mighty God we have," they may have said.

That "sit back and let God do it" attitude can easily become popular, but let us read on to see what else God had to say.

"Be strong and of good courage, do not fear nor be afraid of them..."

"Why of course not, God" they might have thought, "Why would we have to be afraid if you are going to do all the fighting? We'll be on the hill watching ...er ... won't we?"

He goes on to say: "... *For the Lord your God, He is the One who goes with you. He will not leave you nor forsake you."* (verse 6)

"Wait a minute, "you're now saying **"WITH US"**, But Lord, just a moment ago You said You were going **BEFORE** us".

"Well I guess it's not too bad. At least He's **with** us. I can picture God just a little ahead and me marching in right behind Him, with my hand on His shoulder. That's still not too bad."

Don't jump to any conclusions yet — the message goes on in verse 7:

"Be strong and of good courage, for you must go with this people to the land which the Lord has sworn to their fathers to give them, and you shall cause them to inherit it."

"Us Lord ?"

"We have got to go in and take the land? Lord I am not too sure now if I like this army. First of all You said You'd go in; then it sort of changed to You'd go with us; but now the bottom line reality is that, WE must take the land. I don't know if this is the kind of army I want to be in."

The same principle is followed by us today and there is a need for the new testament Guerrilla force to realize its role. God goes ahead of us preparing the way for our victory as a result of prayer and intercession. He certainly does go with us, but we, the army, must be prepared to go and take the targets that the Lord has prepared for us. We are not just a group of people waiting around to get to heaven while God does all the work on our behalf.

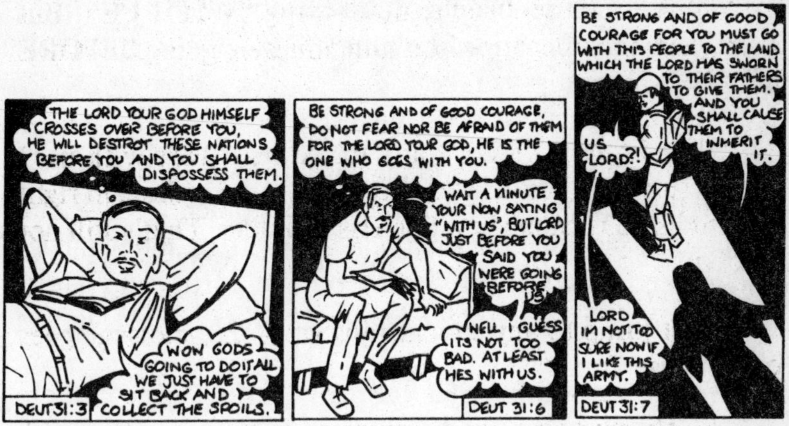

JESUS WILL DO IT!

During World War II the Japanese took over the Philippines and General MacArthur, head of the allied forces, made the now famous statement: "I SHALL RETURN."

He did return and was given full recognition for the victory. The question is, did General MacArthur attack the Philippines alone and single handed? Can you picture General MacArthur, grenades hanging all over him, guns slung around his body, charging in and personally taking every village, every mountain, every valley?

Of course not, his army took every inch of the island. He stood back in a commander's role, giving instructions directing how the war should go.

The army did the work, but history records that General MacArthur took the Philippines; he received the glory and credit.

When I hear statements today like:
"Jesus is going to take China!"
"Jesus is going to take India!"
"Jesus is going to take Australia!"

I can do nothing but wholeheartedly agree. Like General MacArthur, General Jesus is our Commander. He is seated in heavenly places at the right hand of God, planning tactics and giving orders to His army on the earth, and He is *"waiting till His enemies are made His footstool".* (Hebrews 10:13)

Why is He waiting? He has to wait till we the church, realize that our General Jesus is not going to do the work personally. We, His army, are to destroy His enemies and take countries for Him. He's waiting for (other translations say "expecting") — His enemies to be made His footstool.

Who will do the taking? — Obviously we the army!

Who will get all the credit and glory? — Our Commander Jesus.

Spiritual history and the annals in heaven will record that Jesus took the nations. The saints will have victory after victory, but will turn and give Him all the praise and glory.

THE BEGINNING OF THE WAR

Let's go back to the initiator and founder of this new army and try to understand what He was trying to achieve. Only after knowing the reason for the war can we understand our involvement and the role we are to play.

If we ask Christians why Jesus came to earth, the answers would be many and varied:

"To die for sin."

"To heal the sick."

"To feed the hungry."

"To shed His blood."

Each answer would be in part correct, but there is an overall purpose or goal for His coming.

"... For this purpose the Son of God was manifested, that He might destroy the works of the devil." (1 John 3:8)

His mission was to destroy every work of the devil and bring His rule over the lives of men and women.

Let us see what works He destroyed.

He healed the sick, cleansed the lepers, quelled storms, fed the hungry and conquered sin.

He declared war on all the devil's works, and wants them removed from the face of the earth and replaced it with His rule of love, peace and joy. This was an open declaration of war on satan, the god of this age. Jesus was the initiator and demonstrator of this new unconventional guerrilla type of warfare.

Obviously, however, one man could not get to every person on the earth and achieve this goal. An army was needed. Recruits whom He could raise up and train to continue destroying the devil's works as He had done.

These people would need to be loyal believers who would do whatever they were commanded.

He told them: *"Most assuredly I say unto you, he who believes in Me, the works that I do he will do also; . . . "* (John 14:12)

This small initial band of men was trained by Jesus and then it too went out and began this kind of warfare as well.

Again, it was obvious — the numbers to reach were too great, the harvest plenteous and the labourers few. Jesus increased the number to 70 believers who would declare war on the devil, and He even re-emphasized their mission to them. God had sent Him on a mission to destroy the devil's works.

"... As the Father has sent Me, I also send you." (John 20:21)

YOU ARE AT WAR

On leaving the earth to assume His Commander-in-Chief role at heavenly headquarters, His final order was to increase the army to a size where it was able to reach every person in the whole world.

"Go therefore and make disciples of all the nations, ... teaching them to observe all things that I have commanded you..." (Matthew 28:19-20)

The "observe all things" did not mean just to "look at".

The N.I.V. version of the Bible translates it: *"Teaching them to obey all the things I have commanded you."*

It meant to teach others to **DO** all the things that Jesus commanded them to do.

The early Guerrillas did the works that Jesus did — preaching, healing and casting out demons. Then they taught the others to obey and do exactly the same thing.

That early army "observed" the guerrilla tactics and duplicated their actions, and it resulted in a great wave of devil destroying works breaking out across the land. Their action and power became feared so that they became known as the ones who turned the world upside down! In fact, it was satan's world that was being upended and being replaced with God's rule.

Unfortunately, within a few short generations, the war and power had lost their initial surge.

The army just became "observers" of others. It began only to talk of the great work that other people were doing. These "observers" then trained others to be "observers", who trained further observers, who then trained further observers ...

This continued down through the centuries until today, when we still have a great number observing and reporting while a relative few go out to do battle.

RESTORATION TIME

We can look around the earth today and see that there are still many works of the devil to be destroyed. God is looking for His army of believers to rise up and turn satan's world upside down again. The original Guerrillas did it and it will be done again.

Already it has begun in the world. In China there are great stories of revival and destruction of the devil's works. In Africa, hundreds of thousands are being taken out of the hands of the enemy.

We have seen great beginnings of the war in India. As we have preached, lepers have been healed, cripples have walked and the blind have seen. All the signs of devil destruction are there.

When you turn the devil's world upside down, he reacts.

In one town, in direct opposition to our "JESUS HEALS" crusades, the muslims came out and plastered the city with "ALLAH HEALS ALL" posters. It was a hollow crusade against us. They were just talking about healing. We were demonstrating it.

At our recent crusades, the communists became upset and distributed leaflets right around the city, warning people not to come to our meetings. They plastered signs on our vehicles, "CHRISTIANS GO HOME". We, however, gave them an opportunity at the crusade. We invited those unsaved who were deaf and dumb and lepers onto the platform and challenged the communists to come and show how their philosophies could help these people. There was no response. The communists kept very quiet.

We prayed in the name of Jesus Christ and in full view of the huge crowd, Christ demonstrated through their healing that He alone has the answers for today's problems.

We have taken Indian students from our training college at Faith Centre out on crusades into hostile villages, and when God's power was manifest in healing, rioting has broken out in an attempt to try and stop the Word going forth. Our vehicles and equipment were smashed. We continued to preach after the mayhem and Jesus was victorious with salvation and healing following. We rejoice in the fact that like Joshua, our God has gone ahead and prepared the way for us; we needed only to follow in and to possess the land.

Oh, we are at war! We live in exciting times.

God is looking for His Guerrilla force to believe that we can rise up and do the works that Jesus did. His goal is not only third world nations, but every nation, to be turned upside down, and for everyone in the world to be reached.

SONG SUBSTITUTE

Because many have been unaware that they are supposed to be at war and thought they were to be just observers, many potential Guerrillas have been relegated to the role of songsters.

We sing songs like: — "Onward Christian soldiers, marching as to war."

"What war," may I ask?

"Er... well ... I'm not too sure, brother," one may say, "but that song sure stirs my heart."

"Yes, but what war?"

"Er ... well... I guess the man who wrote it use to go to ... er ... war"

That's right. The song writer had a true picture of what Christians are supposed to be doing.

What about the more recent favourite: "God's got an army, marching through the land."

"Yes brother, another great song."
"Well, where is it?"
"Where's what?"
"God's army marching through the land?"

"Well brother ... we're not too sure, but ...er... two weeks ago, we sang that song and the whole church marched around the sanctuary twice. It was a glorious time. We were all so excited."

"Excuse my scepticism, but did the devil get scared ?"

NO CONDEMNATION

At one time I used to get under condemnation about singing those songs.

"Everlasting joy and gladness in my heart

And in that army ... I .. er (cough, splutter)

have got a ... part."

Jesus doesn't only want sounds ... He wants action!

Both my hypocrisy and condemnation soon vanished when the Lord showed me that each tune was prophetic. Each song referred to the army that now is, and is being raised up.

Faith comes by hearing, and hearing by the Word of God. And the Lord showed me that as we sing these songs, faith to be part of the new army was being raised in the saints. The only rebuke the Lord gave me was that Christians were not to picture some army of the past or someone else in the future. It was also not to be a picture of tens of thousands of believers all marching in a regimented line across the land, but an army of Guerrillas making raids and small scale attacks preaching, healing, casting out spirits on a daily basis. Reaching out from their home base and inflicting daily defeat on the devil and all his works as they meet the unsaved in their normal lifestyle.

These war songs are a personal prophecy to each saint.

Can we begin to do it saints, see ourselves as the army every time we sing it.

Let the words of each song be an inspiration of faith to lift your spirit. Then as you sing each week with the new belief rising in your being, it won't be long before your new heart for warfare will lift you into the higher realm of His purpose for our lives.

JESUS NEEDS YOU!

Chapter 4

WAR OR PEACE MOVEMENT?

We are in the midst of a time when the whole world is calling for "PEACE". Rallies and meetings insisting on DISARMAMENT, NON ALIGNMENT, PEACEFUL CO-EXISTENCE and ARMS CONTROL are constantly filling news headlines.

The church to a large degree has caught the spirit of this plea and is apparently happy to live in peaceful co-existence with the devil's works.

Ecclesiastes 3 tells us that there are seasons and timings in God:

"To everything there is a season,
A time for every purpose under heaven:
A time to love
And a time to hate;
A time of war,
And a time of peace" (verses 1 and 8)

"That's the season we live in now; a time of peace," many would say. "God wants us to live in peace."

The church in Moses' time was faced with a similar situation; they were at "peace" wandering around the desert for 40 years. It was not God's will for them to be at peace; **they** had chosen it.

He had told them to go to war, to take the promised land. Only after defeating those possessing their inheritance could they live in the fullness and peace that God had designed for them. The majority of the men sent out to spy out the land gave a "thumbs down" report. Instead of fighting for a better life style, they decided to live a non-aggression existence in the desert. They had their "peace", but were well short of the great promises that God had for them.

Their only thrill of the day was the McManna burger for breakfast, lunch and dinner. They grumbled and complained and thought how much better off they had been in Egypt before God had saved them.

Many of us today can shake our heads and realise how silly they were. If only they had stepped out, believed God and gone to war.

Today, however, we are faced with a similar situation, and have not learned the lesson. Many of God's army have opted for a civilian lifestyle, living in a desert of peace, which produces frustration and grumbling. They know God has something more for them, and don't know why they can't achieve it. Their spiritual experience is so hum-drum and dry in comparison to the rivers of life that they read about in God's Word.

Many look longingly back at the lifestyle before they were "saved", and because of the lack of joy in their Christian experience, they are continually drawn back into Egypt.

God wants His message of the Gospel of His Kingdom preached to every person in this world, and the devil's works destroyed. He has given a promise to "he who believes on Me" to enable us to achieve this.

"Most assuredly, I say to you, he who believes in Me, the works that I do he will do also; and greater works than these he will do, because I go to My Father." (John 14:12)

In the past we have had theological spies walk all over this promised land scripture and come back with a negative report.

"...But it's gigantic! ... We couldn't possibly do it! ..."

"It's a great promise in God's Word ... but, we are not able."

But, praise God, in the midst of the negativity there have been some theological Joshuas and Calebs who confess "We are well able!"

God is looking for the Joshua spirit to rise up within the church, believe God's promise and begin acting on it. He is looking for those who want to get out of the defeatist, peace, desert situation and rise up.

Other theological intelligence gatherers have almost by-passed the main issue of the promise.

"Brother Stuart," one man asked me once, "what do you believe the greater things are ?"

I thought for a second then said: "I don't care!"

"Whatever do you mean?" he queried with a concerned look on his face. "I'm a trainee disciple learning to preach, heal and cast out demons at the same level as Jesus did," I retorted.

"I'm sure by the time I'm doing Jesus' works, I may have the revelation on what the greater things are."

Let us not get side tracked with deep discussion and thought on the "maybe's" and lose the main point of the scripture. Let's go on with the immediate job of at least doing the works that Jesus did. The greater things will then look after themselves.

The main issue here is: what are we choosing to do? We can be like the kind of people under Moses who live in peace, but fall very far short of the blessings and life-style that God has for us.

However, we can have the mind of the new Joshua people who, with that warlike spirit, went on to witness great victories through their God.

We live in exciting times. MOSES IS DEAD — JOSHUA LIVES !

WHAT ABOUT "PEACE" ?

"Surely brother," you may say, "Jesus came as a man of peace and we are supposed to act like Him ?"

Let us see what Jesus has to say about that.

"Do you suppose that I came to give peace on earth? I tell you, not at all but rather division." (Luke 12:51)

His goal was destruction of the devil's works!

"Do not think that I came to bring peace on earth. I did not come to bring peace but a sword." (Matthew 10:34) Jesus knew that he could not be at peace with an enemy who was an aggressor.

Peaceful co-existence is only a short term proposition if you have an enemy that wants to conquer you.

Do you really believe that the devil wants peace and is willing to live in peaceful co-existence with the church? He's not too bright and can't spell too well, and the only peace he wants is:

A piece of your health!

A piece of your money!
A piece of your joy!
A piece of your family!
AND A PIECE OF YOUR PEACE!

He also has a goal and strategy for the earth. Jesus tells us what the devil's outrageous and sinister plan is in John 10:10: *"The thief does not come except to steal, and to kill, and to destroy ..."*

The devil has a crazed obsession to hurt, maim and destroy the people on the earth.

Trying to live in peaceful co-existence with that mentality is just not possible. In contrast to that, Jesus gives His goal which will happen as the devil's works are destroyed:

" ... I have come that they may have life, and that they may have it more abundantly." (John 10:10b)

Jesus has given us a greater power through Him to destroy the hurts and destruction perpetrated on the people of this world.

Real and perpetual peace can only be achieved when all our enemies are defeated and put underfoot. As we have already said in Hebrews 10:13, Jesus is: *"... Waiting till His enemies are made His footstool."*

The warlike side of the Christian is further exemplified in these scriptures:

"And from the days of John the Baptist until now the Kingdom of heaven suffers violence, and the violent take it by force." (Matthew 11:12)

You saints who take the Kingdom are called violent. Yes, its correctly translated from the Greek word "biostes", and the active form of the word is used in the following scripture:

"The law and the prophets were until John. Since that time the Kingdom of God has been preached, and everyone is pressing (entering violently) into it." (Luke 16:16)

Everyone who is taking the Kingdom is not a man of peace, but violent, pressing and forceful.

SPIRITUAL SCHIZOPHRENICS ?

"But brother," you may say, "I have been taught to be loving and peaceful."

Well, the Bible says you are to be violent.

"That sounds contradictory. I can't be violent and loving. I'd be double minded. I can't be both, or I would end up some kind of SPIRITUAL SCHIZOPHRENIC!

Didn't Jesus have compassion on the oppressed ? Surely He was not some kind of Jekyll and Hyde !"

Let's have a little test to see how loving and peaceful you really are. Imagine you are cleaning up in the kitchen and looking into your backyard. You see your beautiful, four year old daughter. She has big eyes, shining hair and everyone in the neighbourhood just adores her. She is the apple of your eye. Suddenly, into your yard races a large black dog. Its eyes are crazed and foam is running from its mouth. It sinks its fangs into your daughter's arm and begins to rip and tear her. Blood begins to gush out of the wound. She looks towards you and screams out.

... "D-a-d-d-y ... D-a-d-dy!"

What do you do ?

Remember, now, you are a loving peaceful Christian!

Obviously, with that in mind, you would calmly sink slowly down on to your knees, put your hands together and pray ...

"Lord, if it be Thy will..."

Well, I don't know about you, but I would definitely fail that peace test. If I didn't have my biggest pair of boots on, they would be on in a flash. I would race down to the yard, grab that dog by the throat and give it the greatest kick I could.

"But brother Stuart," you might say. "that's not peaceful and loving!"

"That poor doggie."

Yes, you are exactly right. It is not peaceful. It is called violence. I am sure that you or any other parent who cared for his or her child would do exactly the same.

The big question is: what was the motivation for my violence?

... the answer ... LOVE!

I could not stand to see her suffering. The love of my child drove me to attack that animal.

My love motivated me to violence.

Our Father God looked down from His heavenly window and saw His children, His creation, being attacked by that wild animal, the devil. He saw us ravaged with sin, sickness, poverty and disease. He heard the cries of His children's pain.

"Daddy ... Daddy ... help us!"

What did He do ?

"For God so loved the world that he sent Jesus Christ" ... For what purpose ... To destroy the works of that mad dog, the devil.

Many Christians today watch sickness and disease tearing others apart. They are dropping to their knees and praying, "Lord if it be thy will."

Jesus only did the will of the Father, and He destroyed sickness and disease wherever He found it.

Can we begin to see the two sides of Jesus now?

He has so much love and compassion on those hurting, that it drove Him to violence to destroy the works of the devil.

THE WORKS THAT JESUS DID SHALL WE DO ALSO!

We are to have so much love and compassion on those afflicted in this world that we are stirred to war and violence to do something about them.

When a soldier enlists for battle, there are two emotive forces that are instilled in him. Firstly, a love for those whom he is defending; and secondly, a hatred for the enemy. This love-hate combination will see him fight his hardest and best.

HOLY HORROR

The reality of this violent side of me hit me between the eyes on my first trip to India. Lepers whose bodies were eaten away looked up helplessly into my eyes; I could almost see the person inside that body crying out: "Daddy, Daddy, help Me!"

I became so annoyed with the rotten disease, I screamed out, "Devil, I'm going to destroy your works!"

Another woman came up to me, her chest so eaten away by cancer, that bones were exposed. An anger arose in me. "Devil I'm going to destroy your works!"

A man approached me with elephantiasis. His leg was grotesquely blown up to four times its normal size. He dragged that leg up and looked at me pleadingly.

It released my spontaneous cry.

"Devil, I'm going to destroy your works!"

Oh, it has been a blessing to see these afflictions destroyed in the Name of Jesus Christ. Thousands and thousands of the devil's works destroyed, and God's children set free from suffering and hurts.

I have been so honoured being able to be one of God's Guerrillas blasting at the devil's works.

We are told: "Blessed are they that mourn." That doesn't mean you sit in a corner and moan and whine at all the problems in the world. It means we look at sin and its effects and we get a groaning and stirring within ourselves. A HOLY HORROR will develop in us and acts as a catalyst. Not to just sit and cry, "Look at the mess," but get up and do something about it.

Jesus didn't just look and mourn over the earth and say: "What a shambles!" He destroyed the works of the devil.

THE WORKS THAT JESUS DID, SHALL WE DO ALSO.

WAR OR PEACE MOVEMENT?

The devil has very cleverly planted the "PEACE" mentality in the church. Some churches now want to remove any songs from their books that mention anything about war. This "WAR BUSTERS" brigade is going to serve to further quieten the church down to a point where the devil can easily overrun us.

The peace thinking has even crept that far into the church now that whenever there is some catastrophe, famine or some outbreak of sickness, we have turned around, looked up to heaven and said limply: "WHY GOD?"

I can just picture the frustration on the Father's face when we say: "Why don't you do something?"

The devil has so manipulated our thinking that we blame God for the devil's works.

Let's picture General MacArthur training and arming his troops, giving them tactics and sending them to take the Philippines?

The army lands on the beach and finds out the local P.O.W.'s prisoners of war, are being badly treated and tortured by the enemy. Can you imagine them sitting down with long faces and crying out: "Why doesn't MacArthur do something ?"

God sent General Jesus on a mission to show us what to do; he has given us all power and authority in His name. Satan has captured the majority of people in this world. They are his prisoners of war, and he daily mistreats and tortures them with sickness, famine, war and the rest of his works.

God wants the same "violent" attitude towards sin and its effects to rise up within us and go forth setting the world free of its captivity to the devil.

The solution in other words, lies within His army. This "WHY DOESN'T GOD DO SOMETHING" must go!

CASTING FEAR ASIDE

Do not be discouraged. God is trying to give you a new vision. Perhaps you could not see or understand your role before, but it is now time for former truths to be restored.

The truth of violence is going to be a catalyst to see a new explosion of evangelism take place.

One of the greatest hindrances to evangelism has been fear. We have been afraid to go and face people; to witness and pray.

This fear has produced a people who don't "feel led" to go out and witness.

Remember the story of the child and the crazed dog. Under normal circumstances a parent would not want to attack a wild dog. They wouldn't "feel led" either.

A natural fear of the danger would stop them.

But the sight of the blood and the cry for help triggered off something deep within their hearts. That mixture of love and anger made the parents put aside all concern for themselves and all fear disappeared.

The Bible tells us in 1 John 4:18: "... *Perfect love casts out all fear.*"

The sight of hurting people in this world should trigger something deep within our hearts. Their cries from help for areas of sin, sickness and oppression should release a compassion within us. For many, the fear of witnessing would disappear.

Once we can love the sinner and hate and abhor the works on them, that love will cast out the fear and a new ferocity and boldness will begin to emerge.

THE POWER RELEASE

A parent defending his or her child will not even think of the human ability to achieve the task. Fighting a wild dog with no weapon would be beyond the natural ability of most. Many parents have related stories of how a supernatural strength came forth when answering the call of a child in distress.

If God's army would just forget its own natural ability and step forth with the ferocity of an angered parent and preach the gospel, then the supernatural power of God would be released. Signs and wonders with demons being cast out and the sick healed would follow our attack.

CHAPTER 5

THE TARGETS

Every army must have a military objective, or goal. What was Joshua's objective in Canaan? He was to establish a nation that could totally be ruled over by God; a people that would bow their knee to His rule and be obedient to His commandments.

The objective of God's modern day Guerrilas is to take the message that God wishes and will establish His rulership, not just over one small area or country, but over the entire earth. He wants every knee to bow and every tongue to confess Him as Lord and ruler.

For Joshua to fulfill his goal or objective, he didn't take the whole land in a day.

He targeted individual cities and captured them, and one by one, little by little, he began to fulfill God's goal.

GUERRILLA CITIES

God's Guerillas need a new concept of their position and goals.

Jesus said in Matthew 16:18, that He, the Rock, is the foundation on which we rely for our strength, and He tells us the gates of hell shall not prevail against us.

Most of us need a mind renewal in the area of "the gates of hell!" Many conceive of a powerful devil who uses these gates to give us our daily beating. We are continually pounded by the gates, causing us untold problems in our everyday walk.

SMASH — the children get sick.
CRUNCH — I lost my job.
SPLAT — somebody really hurt my feelings.
SLAM — The washing machine broke down.

Day after day, our lot in life seems to be beaten and beaten until we are brought down to our spiritual knees in submission.

"Mind you," we say meekly under the weight of our circumstances "the gates won't prevail ... I'm ... hanging on."

We "prevail" with apparently only two means of escape. Firstly to die physically, or secondly, wait for Jesus to return and take us.

For many the cry is: "Lord Jesus, come soon, I don't think I can hang on much longer."

This is hardly the picture of the "gates" that Jesus was trying to portray. In His day the cities had gigantic walls protecting them from hostile armies. The gates were for daily to and fro access, but when under attack, they would be closed and barred. With the enormity of the walls, the best point of penetration was the gates. Once the gates were taken, the attacking army would sweep in with the relatively simple task of a mopping up operation. Jesus was trying to show us in Matthew 16:18 that satan has areas of control, cities, under his rulership, and they are guarded by gates; the gates of hell.

The "peace" mentality of the church has made us think that we must passively sit and allow these gates to smash us while we bravely hang on.

J.B. Philips translates the passage:

"The gates of hell shall be powerless against the church".

Joshua and his army had a goal to take cities. Could you possibly imagine satan using the city gates like some giant fly swatter, chasing the army around the desert trying to squash them? No! His army stormed gates and took every city controlled by their enemy. The days of our "squashing" must cease. We, as God's army, knowing that the gates of hell are powerless against us, must storm out and take territory and cities presently under satan's control, we must bring them under the government of King Jesus.

WHAT ARE THE CITIES?

When we mention "cities" the majority of us think in terms of places like New York, London and Sydney. Even for the Christians, we think of "taking" our own home town. Again, the majority can picture a great army swarming into the town and taking it.

But our General, Jesus, is not expecting you to take the whole town in a day. God's goal is not geographical areas His goal is people.

Each unsaved person is like a walled city, or kingdom, and his present ruler is the dictator, satan. He exerts his influence and sinister power over their lives and as a result they are a city with many problems. The walls are walls of bondages, surrounding each one of them.

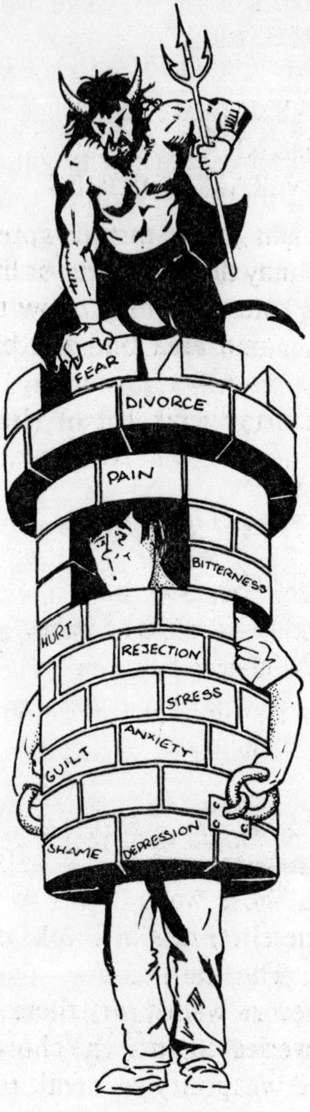
FEAR
DIVORCE
PAIN
BITTERNESS
HURT
REJECTION
STRESS
ANXIETY
GUILT
SHAME
DEPRESSION

WALLS OF SICKNESS
WALLS OF DEPRESSION
WALLS OF SIN
WALLS OF FAMILY PROBLEMS
WALLS OF LONELINESS
WALLS OF FINANCIAL WORRIES

Some unsaved might give an outside appearance that they are not bound. They may drive a big car or live in a big home. But satan is a cruel ruler that may allow them to have an apparent freedom in one area but will bind them up in another.

Joshua and his army took literal cities. Our targets, should we accept the mission, is to take spiritual cities, "individual people".

MISSION IMPOSSIBLE?

Many have looked at the walls of bondages and wondered if certain people could ever be saved.

"My Boss, oh, all he thinks about is money. He has dollar signs on his eyelids. The walls; the walls are impossible to breach."

"Not Uncle Fred, he's the crankiest thing on two legs, mention God and he'll bite your head off."

Getting through those walls is out of the question.

"Not that old derelict, he's a drunk and smells."

"The walls ... The walls ... !"

Remember, for every walled city there is a way in. The gates of hell are powerless against the church, because God has provided us the weaponry to break through.

God does not want us to see the walls, but to see the person imprisoned inside by satan. He wants us to see inside a potential saint who has been hurt and broken down by circumstances brought about by their present leader.

His campaign to kill, steal from them and destroy them has brought them to a point of total frustration and depression on many occasions.

They know they have bondages and secretly have cried out to God.

"God, I'm a millionaire, but my family life is a mess. God help me."

"Lord, I know I'm a cantankerous old thing, but so many people have hurt me. Please help me."

"God I know I'm an alcoholic but I want to get out of it. If you are really there, have mercy on me."

So many have pleaded with God, but because apparently He didn't hear their cry, they became embittered, and in frustration, finally said: "There can't be a God, He wouldn't allow this if He were real."

The problem, as we have already discussed, was not God. The solution of course lies in the hands of the church. He has commanded the church to destroy the works of the devil, by using the spiritual weapons He has provided.

We are to see the plight of the one trapped inside these walls, and the compassion to see them set free will motivate us to destroy the bondages surrounding their lives.

Our enemy is not people.

CELL

DEFENSIVENESS

Our fight is against the devil's works, the bondages in their lives.

Our enemies are not hindus, muslims, communists or humanists, but the spiritual forces deceiving and holding them.

"For we do not wrestle against flesh and blood, but against principalities, against powers, against the rulers of the darkness of this age, against spiritual hosts of wickedness in the heavenly places." (Ephesians 6:12)

We are to love the "flesh and blood", the person, and destroy the works and powers influencing his or her life.

This is where our "love" message has gone astray. God does not expect you to "love" the devil's works. We love the person inside the prison walls and hate the walls of bondage. This was the love Jesus exhibited when He was crucified: *"Father, forgive them, for they do not know what they do."* (Luke 23:34) He realizes the devil's works, his power and influence had blinded them. His love did not cease for them, but His hatred for the devil's works was equally unceasing.

WAR AT HOME

After returning from India to my homeland of Australia, I realized how I had almost signed a non-aggression pact with the devil. Seeing leprosy in India had raised a violence in me over there, but I soon realized a different form of leprosy was rampant in my own nation.

Drugs, prostitution, pornography, alcoholism, abortion, homosexuality and all the associated by-products; divorce, A.I.D.S., hurt people, are all part of western leprosy.

I realized in the past I didn't have the same aggression towards these as the physical problems in India, and have subtly been tricked into a 'peace' mentality towards them.

"That's the way our society is today," or "After all, it is end times", we have been told.

No, they are all the devil's works, and we cannot simply live in peaceful coexistence with them. They all need to be destroyed. We need to get the same violence and anger towards any work of the devil as we would towards leprosy and want to see it removed from people's lives.

GET THE ROOT

This does not necessarily mean running around holding protest marches, displaying placards and getting laws changed trying to force Kingdom standards on others.

I remember in my mother's garden, there was a noxious bush called Lantana. You could cut the branches of that thing year after year and it would grow back even stronger.

Many Christians have been trimming the branches of alcoholism, abortion and drug addiction by cutting the branches. Our own legislators have helped by laws and jail sentences and we keep the tree trimmed. I praise God for the past work of those who have stood for righteousness and trimmed the branches. The majority of Christians have stood back and watched as the few stood up.

As we cut back that Lantana year after year, I became more and more annoyed with it. The only answer was the root had to come out. It meant initially a little more hard work, but the final result would mean no more trimming.

The root of all our western ills lies in the leadership of every unsaved person. Satan influences their heart decision. Not until the homosexuals, prostitutes and porno kings change rulers and be governed by Jesus Christ can the root of the problems be solved.

Can we begin to get annoyed with the continued re-appearance of the branches of abortion, A.I.D.S. and our other leprous ills?

Can we get that outraged we are prepared to put in a little extra labour and destroy the root of the problem?

God is raising a people who will be able to destroy the root of the problem. He is raising his army of "devil destroyers" today and HE NEEDS YOU.

LITTLE BY LITTLE

We can look at our entire nation or even our own hometown and almost surrender because of the apparent enormity of the task.

However, Joshua gives us again the tactic — he took the whole area, one city at a time. They were told that they would take the land little by little.

You may only witness to one person a week. Others may set themselves to have more encounters. Can you imagine the effect if everyone in your church captured only one city a week? That would be the greatest revival in your city's history!

God is now waiting for us to begin individual guerrilla strikes on one city at a time. One by one, little by little we can take whole nations for our Leader. What an exciting life God has opened for you.

We under the better covenant have the joy and thrill of capturing people, our spiritual "cities", and seeing them surrender under the rulership of Jesus Christ.

SPIRITUAL "PUMP UP"

We have to change our picture of our present Christian stance.

For many, Sunday is the last day of the week.

"What do you mean by that ?" you may ask.

Well, many of us have spent the week being beaten thumped and smashed by the gates of hell all week.

Monday: Burnt my fingers on the toaster.
Tuesday: My best friend let me down.
Wednesday: The day off sick.
Thursday: Argument with the family.
Friday: My boss chewed me out.
And just to top off the week, on Saturday, I dented the car.

Many of us are so depressed after six days, that we feel as spiritually low as a deflated balloon. We crawl into church on our spiritual knees expecting the solution to our weekly mauling.

The answer — Yes, Sunday is the day of our weekly "PUMP UP".

We come to church and we say in our hearts: "Oh yes song leader, sing some songs that will get me lifted." We stand and wait for them to take us to heavenly heights and after rejoicing in song we are feeling a little more inflated.

Now the message: "Oh yes Pastor, something that will really give me a lift today please."

The pastor then pumps out a great inspiring message which you eagerly take in.

The "pump up" has done its required task and you walk out of church spiritually bulging and now ready to face another week of continual deflating circumstances.

The gates of hell then do a repeat performance on you for the next six days, and by Sunday, the treatment needs to be re-administered.

The ups and downs of life go on and on.

Six days of deflation — the seventh day a "pump up".

Six days of deflation — the seventh day a "pump up".

Six days of deflation — the seventh day a "pump up".

If you are really lucky you manage to get a bit of mouth to mouth resuscitation at mid-week home fellowships.

SUNDAY IS NOT THE LAST DAY OF THE WEEK! ITS THE FIRST!

On Sunday we are supposed to come to church and sing our songs like "God's got an Army" and "Onward Christian Soldiers" and we declare openly who we are and what our task is.

The next six days we march out and select individual people (our cities), declare war, and destroy the devil's works and release that prisoner from the power of satan.

The following Sunday the pastor would not have to squeeze out a testimony by asking: "Can anyone share what Jesus has done in their lives this week ... er ... anyone?"

He would be flooded by people wishing to give their reports on how the war went. Can you imagine 50 people giving a one-minute testimony, front line report of demonic casualties.

"Mrs Jones was saved at at the supermarket!" "My Uncle Fred was healed of arthritis!" "A man at work accepted Christ and was healed!" "A potential divorce case was nullified!"

After 50 minutes of hearing the effect of aggressive warfare, others would be lifted by the contagious excitement and want to go to war themselves. The pastor would not even need to preach that day.

If that happened to us every week, we wouldn't come to church battle scarred looking for a pump up.

We'd come to church so pumped up from our victories that we would spontaneously break into praise and worship for the great things He had done in the last week and the devil destruction ahead of us for the next six days.

That's how I believe the early church operated and turned the world upside down.

At the end of each week they came together to have a real celebration of what Jesus Christ had done for them.

God is wanting to see it happen today right across the earth, and you, God's Guerrillas, are going to be part of it.

CHAPTER 6

BASIC TRAINING — BOOT CAMP

In the book of Joel, we are told of another army of God and from these scriptures, we can find principles of warfare that will assist our modern day God's Guerrillas.

For the raising of Joel's army, this declaration was given; *"... Prepare for war! Wake up the mighty men, let all the men of war draw near. Let them come up. Beat your plowshares into swords and your pruninghooks into spears; Let the weak say, I am strong."* Joel 3:9-10

I have preached in many churches on God's "mighty men" going to war. I can almost read many of the minds of those listening to the message:

"Yes! Those mighty men should rise up and fight! ... whoever they are!"

We have failed to realize that we, the church, the majority of those presently seated in pews, are the mighty men and women of God.

God is presently blowing His trumpet of warfare. He has men, (His trumpets) carrying His message, sounding an alarm for preparation for war.

What does an alarm clock do to you early in the morning? It shakes you out of the beautiful peaceful bliss you have been in and wakes you up to the start of a new day.

God's alarm is a beautiful sound for a new day in the church.

However, to what are we being awakened? I'm sure the majority are already awake to the fact of the need for more evangelism and outreach. That's not what the alarm is all about. The trumpet blast is to wake you up to the fact that **you are the mighty men** and you need to get prepared.

LACK OF ABILITY?

Right now you may be stirred in your spirit to be involved, to want to go and do some devil destroying, but you sense a lack of ability in your life.

"Who me?" you might retort. "Why, obviously you don't know me very well. I'm too weak to be a mighty man or woman of God."

That's why the scripture goes on to say: "Let the weak say I am strong". You cannot do it in your own strength, but by learning how to release God's power that is already in you, you can be a mighty person.

"Yes," you may say, "I've heard it before, but it just hasn't worked out for me."

A frustration has crept into many parts of the church.

Many have woken up in the past and marched out to do battle. The majority of these fell flat on their faces, failed miserably under fire, and crawled back into camp shot down in flames. No signs and wonders confirmed their word, no cities taken.

PREPARE WAR !

The problem is apparent, but the solution rather obvious. In a conventional army, the troops are not expected to go out and face the enemy without training. Otherwise they'd be easily defeated. Can you imagine a soldier going to war not knowing how to use his rifle and grenades? Similarly, within the ranks of God's Guerrillas the lack of knowledge, and more importantly skill in the use of our weapons of warfare, has seen us defeated time and time again.

Notice that Joel's army was not told to go out and start fighting the same day. "PREPARE WAR!" was the order given.

"Prepare War!" means exactly that! Get ready! Be trained! A conventional army goes through basic training or "boot camp". During this course every recruit learns how to take orders and use his basic weapons, his rifle and grenades.

When you accepted Jesus as Lord, whether you realized it or not, you enlisted in His army. Jesus Christ is now your Commanding Officer.

THE WEAPON OF ENTHUSIASM

When you first joined up, you probably ran around "on fire" telling your friends and relatives of your experience and possibly seeing some results. After a while, however your enthusiasm waned. There were too many failures, too much opposition through which you couldn't win. Other Christians watched and waited with a knowing smile that you would eventually "burn out" just as they did and that you would eventually join the status quo of "burnt out veterans."

God's purpose is not to let you or any others burn out. We must realize that if we are going to see revival, it's no use going out armed only with the weapon of enthusiasm.

Our Commander has a training programme, a "boot camp" for you to learn the weapons of your warfare to use in addition to your enthusiasm to enable you to be fired up and continually burn on.

BASIC OFFENSIVE WEAPONS

For every trainee Guerrilla there are basic weapons which he needs to know how to use. A list of three of these offensive weapons is found in Mark 16:15-18:

WEAPON I — The preaching of the Gospel of the Kingdom.

WEAPON II — Casting out of demons.

WEAPON III — Laying hands on the sick.

These weapons are available to "those who believe", and all believing recruits can be trained in their use. These are three of your basic offensive weapons, your rifle and grenades so to speak.

At a boot camp in the natural army, everybody who joins the army gets trained. Nobody misses out on basic training.

Even the cook goes through the course.

Once I could not see the sense in that. Why train a cook to fire a rifle? Surely the closest he would come to hand-to-hand combat would be beating eggs!

I realized however that the enemy can infiltrate behind the front lines and get into the kitchen. If that cook doesn't know how to fire his rifle ... he's had it!

Every Christian needs to learn to use his basic weapons, as the enemy will try at some stage to get behind your lines.

He will try to bring his weapons of sickness and disease into your home, your family and even your own body.

If you don't know how to shoot your spiritual rifle and throw your holy hand grenades, you'll be in big trouble and find yourself surrendering to the devil instead of him fleeing from you.

I'M ABOVE SOLDIERING

Many have thought "their ministry" did not include guerrilla warfare and so did not need basic training.

"But I'm an intercessor," one may say. God bless you for your intercession, but get your basic training.

"Well, I'm a musician!" others may retort. Praise God for your song and musical talents.

But you need your basic training.

Even members of the military band go through "boot camp". They have the good sense to realize that the enemy will try to kill anybody in the opposition army.

The devil likewise will attack anyone in God's army, he knows who you are and has a programme to kill, steal and destroy.

Every Christian needs to be trained and have a foundational ministry of these offensive weapons. Of course He certainly does use other talents and spiritual giftings in addition to this grassroots ministry, and these are discussed in later chapters.

OUR OFFICERS WILL SAVE US

Many of us have looked to our leaders to defend us when the enemy has attacked, but it's time for the church to grow up and learn to defend ourselves. Your pastor cannot be riding shotgun for you every moment of the day. What will happen to you if the enemy strikes and you can't contact him?

The Lord wants all housewives, accountants, plumbers, secretaries, cooks and musicians — all CHRISTIANS — firstly to defend themselves and their own families, and secondly, offensively reaching out around your neighbourhood and work places, setting the unsaved free. A growing church means growing people, people who are growing up to do the works that Jesus did. This will leave more time for the pastor to devote time on the new baby Christians coming into the church as a result of your efforts. Numerical growth automatically comes as we do the works that Jesus did.

A NATION AT WAR !

If a country or nation goes to war, a combined "WAR EFFORT" of the government and the people moves into action. They have a common goal and purpose to see the enemy defeated, with all available financial resources and manpower directed to that end.

Automobile manufacturers turn out tanks.

Fashion houses make uniforms.

Sporting goods firms produce machine guns.

Civilians give surplus funds for war bonds.

This was the attitude God was trying to stir up in Joel's army.

"Beat your plowshares into swords and your pruning hooks into spears"

In other words, turn your peace time equipment into equipment that can complement the war effort.

The church is one people, a HOLY NATION under God. I believe that God is calling us to be one nation in HIS war effort.

The early Guerrillas had this warlike mentality, they gave their lives and finances for the WAR EFFORT.

If we really believe that Jesus meant it when He commanded that "every creature" hear the good news, and if we understand our part in the war, a few commitments need to be made.

It may mean a sacrifice in finances and of your time to achieve that end. It may mean that some of your "peace" projects will need to be deferred. It may mean you give more of yourself for boot camp training. Or if you are trained, more of your manpower in the field.

No country ever goes to war without a final goal for peace. The purpose for fighting is for peace. Isaiah talks of a time when we will have such a time:

"... They shall beat their swords into plowshares,
And their spears into pruning hooks;
Nation shall not lift up sword against nation
Neither shall they learn war anymore." (Isaiah 2:4)

But that end has not been reached as yet.

"And this gospel of the kingdom will be preached in all the world as a witness to all the nations, and then the end will come." (Matthew 24:14)

Somebody once said. "But hasn't that happened hundreds of years ago?" "Well, Jesus told us to be as little children and so I always ask a childlike question:

"If that scripture has been fulfilled ... WHY HASN'T THE END COME?"

The goal of preaching to "every creature" needs to be accomplished. Remember we are just beginning our eternal lives. God is requiring a small war effort now as a part of our eternal and everlasting peace.

I believe our WAR EFFORT, although it seems large now, is insignificant in the whole picture of peace and new life that lies ahead of us.

"Eye has not seen, nor ear heard,
Nor have entered into the heart of man
the things which God has prepared for those who love Him."
(1 Corinthians 2:9)

CHAPTER 7

A SECOND TRUMPET?

At present there are many men of God, His trumpets, blasting out a message of holiness in the church. Simultaneously, as we previously mentioned, there is a trumpet call for restored weaponry and power to enable us to go to war.

Now which of these trumpets are we to heed? Both seem to have truth but appear to pull the believers totally into either one camp of holiness or the other camp of power.

I can remember as a younger Christian, being a little confused and torn between visiting ministries as they gave out "THE MESSAGE FOR THE HOUR." One would raise in me great expectations in faith and my ability to do all things through Christ who strengthens me. The next week I would find myself totally repentant and disgusted with myself as the holiness preacher shook the church. For weeks after I would be in fear and trepidation trying to present myself as a sanctified vessel and totally forgetting about doing something for God . . . until the next "faith" preacher.

Now what is God trying to say? Is it holiness or power? Is God trying to confuse us, or is possibly one of them a false voice?

ONLY ONE SOUND

Both messages are correct because they are actually one sound. Holiness is part of the message. Power is part of the message. Together they give the whole trumpet call ... TO PREPARE AN ARMY.

We can see the overall picture and bring the balance of both messages when we see God's overall plan. He is presently raising an army which, if it is going to have maximum efficiency, needs two vital qualifications. It needs to be both holy AND powerful.

The word "holiness" brings up thoughts for many of an overawing accomplishment they feel is too great to conquer.

Let's bring holiness down to one simple word "obedience". When our Commanding Officer gives us an order, we are to obey.

In the preparation of a conventional army, training of the use of weapons is critical, but equally important is the ability of the soldier to take orders.

The new recruit is given a uniform and is immediately subjected to stringent discipline:
"Put that cigarette out !"
"Stand up straight !"
"Eyes front !"
"Do fifty push ups !"

However this initial discipline is not the whole purpose of their joining the army. They are expected to do more than to wear a uniform, parade up and down and salute the flag when the national anthem is played. They joined to be trained for a higher purpose and calling.

THEY ARE BEING TRAINED TO FIGHT FOR THEIR COUNTRY AND ITS LEADER.

Unfortunately, many Christians have missed a greater purpose in their calling and think that parading is all there is to church life. As long as they don't smoke, don't drink, wear the uniform of respectability, line up for church each Sunday, sing some songs and put money in the plate, they feel they are fulfilling their role.

Christians are being trained for a higher purpose and calling.

YOU ARE BEING TRAINED TO FIGHT FOR YOUR LEADER, JESUS CHRIST, AND THE ESTABLISHMENT OF HIS KINGDOM.

He is now revealing His purposes to the church that we may be stirred to further action. Many of us formerly were unaware of the greater purpose and saw no further than what we were presently involved in. Praise God it's a new day for you.

LORD AND BOSS

Many of us need to come into a fresh understanding of the meaning of "Lord". Many are calling Him "Lord" but are not being obedient to all His orders. Can you imagine if at work your boss came up to you and said: "Here's a broom, sweep the floor."

You then kneel on the floor, look lovingly and sweetly into his eyes and to the tune of "He is Lord", you sing:

"You're my boss
You're my boss-s-s
You pay my wages
You're my boss

He would probably look you right in the eye and say "Nice song ... nice gesture ..."

"Now if you don't get to work ... you get the sack !"

In other words, you show him he's boss by being obedient to him.

I know our boss Jesus loves the sacrifice of praise from our mouths, but He also wants the church to demonstrate His Lordship with our actions. He wants us to pick up our spiritual brooms and help sweep the devil's works off the face of this earth. I wonder how many of us, but for the grace of God, deserve to get the sack.

"LED" BY OBEDIENCE!

When you are at work, you might not "feel led" to sweep the floor. It is not the most pleasant of tasks.

YOU DO IT THROUGH OBEDIENCE!

When a conventional army goes to war, I'm sure not too many "feel led" either. War is horrible; nobody really "loves" facing and fighting the enemy. Nobody "feels led" to die!

THEY DO IT THROUGH OBEDIENCE!

I'm sure God's Guerrillas don't always want to go out or 'feel led' to go and destroy the devil's works.

THEY DO IT THROUGH OBEDIENCE!

THE PURPOSE OF HOLINESS

The counter-balancing effect of the holiness and obedience message cannot be overstressed to those who want to join God's Guerrillas just for the "shoot up" and the action.

In the traditional army, many new recruits are shaken and mystified by the sudden discipline and initially cannot see the purpose for the regimentation.

"I joined to fight, not to march up and down," might be a typical statement from the inexperienced. As we have just discussed, they are being trained for a higher calling. If they can't be obedient to a simple command to get into line, how would it be possible to be obedient in the thick of battle? Learning to take orders is a basic foundation of any successful army.

Our army handbook, the Bible, gives us the very same principle: *"He who is faithful in the least is faithful also in much, while he who is unreliable in the least is unreliable in much also."* Luke 16:10 Berkeley.

Many potential God's Guerrillas who have wanted to be used on the front lines never lasted very long, simply because they could not take orders and be obedient in the little things.

Timothy was told *"to flee youthful lusts"* (2 Timothy 2:22). Many of us find some disobedient areas in our lives difficult to flee.

Many of us, after hearing a bone shaking message of "Be Holy as I am Holy", are rightly convicted and embark on a course to flee sinful areas and purge them from our lives.

This message has an initial impact and we are able to keep ourselves as a sanctified vessel for some time. For some the effect of the message wears off and we slip back down to our former levels.

"Flee youthful lusts", Timothy was told.

If you are fleeing "FROM" one thing, you must have something else to go "TO".

You must replace your disobedient action areas with obedient action areas. Some people have some idea that to be a holy, sanctified vessel you must be set apart like some monk.

No, God has a calling to fill the void of your past youthful lusts. " ... *If a man keeps himself clean from the contaminations of evil he will be a vessel for honourable purposes, dedicated and serviceable for the use of the master of the household, all ready, in fact, for any good purpose."* (2 Timothy 2:21 J.B. Phillips)

You are not just cleaning yourself up to be a vessel sitting in a corner. God wants to use you for good purposes, and this includes devil destroying.

Being aware of your higher calling can be the stimulus for us and motivate us to lead a life constantly free from the hindrances of sin. A simple example of this can be seen by comparing these two stories.

Story One

Little Johnny aged 7 is playing in a newly found mud puddle just outside his home. His horrified mother sees him covered in mud from head to toe.

"Johnny, get out of that mud, you're a naughty boy," she cries out at the top of her voice.

"Aw Mummy, Do I have to? I've got nothing else to do." he pleads reluctantly.

Now in stronger tones,she says:

"If you don't get out of that mud, I'll be out to you with ... THE STRAP!"

"Aw Mum!"

"I'm going to count to three ... one ... two !"

Johnny now, under threat, stands up with tears in his eyes and saunters back to the house looking back longingly at the mudpool with every step.

He fights and complains in the bathtub as his mother struggles to clean him up ...Johnny will be back in the mudpool tomorrow.

Story Two

Same Johnny, same mud pool.

"Johnny get out of that mud — if I've told you once, I've told you a thousand times."

"Aw mum, it's not fair, I've got nothing else to do!"

"Now listen, daddy wants to take you on a fishing trip with him this afternoon."

"You can't go looking like that. "

"Johnny ... Johnny ... did you hear what I said? "

Johnny can't hear a word. He's already in the bathroom cleaning himself up and getting ready for the expedition with his dad.

YOUR HEAVENLY FATHER WANTS TO TAKE YOU ON A SPIRITUAL FISHING TRIP.

BUT THAT'S A REWARD

Many of us have been playing in the mud of our youthful lusts. God shouldn't have to send ministers of His Word continually around to us with spiritual soap to help clean us up. He wants you to get so excited and motivated about the fishing mission He has for you, that you clean yourself up.

"No one engaged in warfare entangles himself with the affairs of this life, that he may please him who enlisted him as a soldier." (2 Timothy 2:4)

Some may say but that's being good so that we will receive a reward. Yes, that's exactly what it is. As much as we obey because he is our Lord and we want to please him, he promises rewards to those who will be obedient.

"... He is a rewarder of those who diligently seek Him." (Hebrews 11:6)

"Calamity pursues sinners but prosperity rewards the righteous." Prov. 13:21 Berkeley.

God continuously in His Word has wanted us to catch the vision of the rewards for the obedient. Proverbs 29:18 (KJV) tells us that without a vision, the people perish. Many Christians have been perishing, unable to stay free of the mud of sin because of that lack of vision.

CLOGGED EARS

I know, as a young Christian, I was not able to hear God clearly because of certain youthful lusts in my life. I was a bachelor businessman, lived in a penthouse, drove a large Mercedes Benz and because of my position and status in life, I had **my** ideas of what my calling would be. Obviously anything the Lord would want me to do would be in line with the people I presently mixed with or at least of that standard.

If for instance, the Lord said to me: "Go to Hawaii," I would have been right in my element.

"Yes Sir! Commanding Officer, I'm packing right now," would have been my immediate response. That would have been my scene, preaching to beautiful people on sandy beaches.

If on the other hand I had heard a voice "GO TO INDIA," I would have instantly known that there had been a communication mix up, I would have cried out immediately:

"I REBUKE YOU DEVIL!"

Now there is nothing wrong with owning cars, houses and leading a certain lifestyle ... as long as they are not blockages to be able to hear what God is saying.

I ended up in India and have been blessed mightily in ministry for years. The nation has been, and still is, part of my personal "boot camp" with the Lord overseeing my total training programme.

I am not advocating that everyone packs his bags and goes to Africa or India tomorrow, but that we simply put aside anything that would hinder us from hearing our Commander's voice.

GOD COMMUNIQUES

Can you imagine a conventional soldier in the heat of the battle with no radio contact with his officers at home base? He could end up shooting his own men.

General Jesus, oversighting the war from His heavenly headquarters, is constantly attempting to get information and communiques to His army on tactics that will help us defeat our enemy.

However our youthful lusts are causing static and interference with our receivers. Daily guidance, words of knowledge, discerning of spirits and other instructions from our officer can only clearly and continuously be received as we eliminate the static.

Remember what 2 Timothy 2:21 said: "... *If a man keep himself clean from the contaminations of evil, he will be a vessel used for honourable purposes dedicated and servicable for the use of the master of the household, all ready for every good purpose.*"

At present the church is doing SOME good work, but we have a promise from John 14:12 that the works that Jesus did, we shall do also, and greater things shall we do.

Jesus healed the sick, cleansed the lepers, raised the dead, cast out demons.

For those who wish to be fully trained, we must keep ourselves clean from the contaminations so that we can do EVERY good work the Lord would want us to accomplish.

Can you imagine Christian judges, politicians, cleaners, film stars, clerks going to their place of work, exhibiting a godly, holy life and yet giving answers to all the hurting people at their work? Preaching, healing and setting them free. That is the guerilla activity that God is wanting from you.

Chapter 8

ADDITIONAL FIREPOWER

We have established that each Guerrilla carries his own basic offensive weaponry, which includes the preaching of the gospel, the casting out of demons and the laying on of hands. These are his rifle and grenades. However, God has additional weaponry for his troops, a second level of bombardment which can be used to dislodge an extremely resistant enemy.

A complete inventory of the weapons with our code name "gifts of the Spirit" is listed in 1 Corinthians 12:8—11:

1. The word of wisdom
2. The word of knowledge
3. Gift of faith
4. Gifts of healings
5. Working of miracles
6. Gift of prophecy
7. Discerning of spirits
8. Different kinds of tongues
9. Interpretation of tongues

How do these weapons operate supplementary to our basic weapons?

In a conventional army, there may be times in a battle where the enemy troops may have retreated into a strongly fortified building. They are entrenched defensively and normal rifle and grenade power is just not making enough impact.

The commanding officer assessing the situation and realizing additional weaponry is needed, would order heavy artillery to bombard the enemy stronghold. After this "softening up" process, the troops are able to complete a mopping up operation and inflict final defeat using their basic weapons, their rifles and grenades.

An example of this is recorded in the book of Joshua when his army took the city of Jericho. The soldiers were armed with their basic weaponry, their spears and swords.

The citizens of Jericho were well aware of the imminent attack and entrenched themselves behind the huge city walls. *"Now Jericho was securely shut up because of the children of Israel ..."* (Joshua 6:1)

What did Israel's Supreme Commander do? Realizing the daunting task ahead with only spears and swords, God decided to give His army additional assistance with a "softening up" process and gave the walls of Jericho a spiritual bombardment. As we all know, the walls came crashing to the ground and gave the army access for the mopping up operation with their basic weapons.

They went in and inflicted final defeat with their basic weapons. *"And they utterly destroyed all that was in the city ... with the edge of sword."* (Joshua 6:21)

EVANGELISTS' JERICHOS

Many have witnessed these "Jericho" type occurrences happen at the hands of gifted evangelists. Even before preaching, the "gifts" begin to operate as the Holy Spirit gives the evangelist words of knowledge, resulting in walls of bondage being barraged. The blind see, the dumb speak, the cripples walk.

Many of the people healed may never have heard the gospel or had little or no faith for their deliverance. Some may have come to the meeting with a sceptical attitude. God works the bombarding power of the Holy spirit above their faith levels and "Jerichos" occur.

These shock tactics work. Even sceptics at least give an ear to hear. This creates an opportunity for the gospel, (the sword of the Spirit), to be used to complete the capture.

A gifted evangelist friend of mine once had three people from the newspaper at one of his meetings to report on "supposed" healings. Even after seeing some healings they sat there stoney-faced, so he challenged them to come out and let God touch them. The three of them fell flat to the floor, just as I imagined the Jericho walls did. After they got to their feet they were now open to listen to the gospel and I know at least one of them, a young lady, received Jesus as her Saviour as the basic weapon of the sword did its work.

As we know, Joshua's army did not take every city by the Jericho method. Other cities such as Gibeon, Chephirah, Beeroth and Kirath Jearim all surrendered without a fight after hearing about the power of God exhibited at Jericho.

The evangelist does not attack everyone with the "Jericho" method. In fact, usually a comparative few in meetings of thousands will be touched this way.

Remember gifts of healings and working of miracles and other gifts are only operated as the Commander wills.

However, others at the meeting, after seeing the wall-destroying gifts operating, will stand in awe and the reverential fear of God. Once they see the reality of His might and power, they too, like the cities of old, are more than willing to surrender.

The devil's works in their city can now be destroyed by the basic weapons, the preaching of the gospel, the laying on of hands and the casting out of demons.

GUERRILLA JERICHOS — One to one

As much as most of us have not been called to the office of an evangelist and conduct meetings with hundreds or even thousands of people, we still have a warfare to conduct on an individual level.

As we go out to take the unsaved cities on a one to one basis, we may from time to time, encounter a Jericho. These are the kind of people that whenever you mention the Bible, church, or Jesus, they securely shut themselves up and become highly defensive. Our weapons of the gospel seem to bounce off their walls.

Our Commander-in-Chief may assess the situation and order up the gifts of the Spirit (our heavy artillery) which can give us the initial breakthrough. The city can then be taken by our basic weaponry.

While preaching in New Zealand, a Christian friend took me out on Auckland Harbour for a cruise on his boat. There were about six on board, one of them being unsaved. We were engaged in talking of things of the Lord, and as a result, the unsaved man made himself scarce and went to another part of the launch. My friend told me he had preached the gospel to this man many times and the man had consistently resisted. When he entered the cabin once again, the Holy Spirit gave me a word of knowledge about his bad back and the healing to be appropriated by the lengthening of one leg. When I told him this, he was shocked as he was aware that he had the leg problem.

"How did you know that ?" he blurted out.

"The Lord told me," I replied, looking into his now very large eyes.

As I prayed for him and the leg grew, he felt God's power and tears started to appear in his eyes.

The walls were beginning to crumble.

He walked away shaking his head but within a few minutes was back at my side, telling me of the problems in his life. I preached a simple gospel message to him and he surrendered and gave his life to Jesus.

Another city for God's Kingdom.

Do all get saved like that? No. This will happen from time to time, as the Spirit wills, only when He sees it necessary. Of the hundreds I've witnessed to on a one to one basis, only a comparative few have been hit by the artillery method.

The majority have been won by basic weaponry, preaching the gospel to them, raising faith in their hearts for salvation and healing, and then signs and wonders following.

YOUR EXTRA FIREPOWER

In a conventional army after basic training, you are posted to a certain unit or corps. Each one of the corps has a different function which works in with an overall plan of winning the war. Apart from your basic call as a soldier, you will be placed in a functioning position to help our Commander's overall war strategy.

Your giftings chosen by the Holy Spirit *"distributing to each one individually as He wills"* (1 Corinthians 12:11) will be in line with your particular posting.

If for instance you were in the intelligence or counter intelligence corps, you may operate in the word of wisdom, discerning of spirits or the word of knowedge.

These weapons of God's secret service can spy on the activities of the devil and let us know what appropriate offensive tactics we need to take.

Others who have been stationed in communications or signal corps may operate in different kinds of tongues, interpretations of tongues, and prophecy. One of the greatest needs of the army is morale, and so encouragement and exhortation is a great weapon against defeatist propaganda.

Marines, front line soldiers or shock troops are breakthrough men and will need powerful offensive weaponry assistance. Gifts of faith, working of miracles and gifts of healing would be necessary for this type of spiritual soldiering.

Guerrillas who are apostles or front line evangelists frequently see this kind of weaponry in their ministry.

Now God can and does work any gift through any person at any time. Our experience has shown us a predominance of major giftings with occasional experiences of others from time to time.

As an evangelist I often see the word of knowledge and gifts of healing operating. However in the area of prophecy it seemed that I was only just above Balaam's ass in being used. But there have been times when a prophetic word was needed when I was there and God chose to use me.

The main point to remember is that God is not always going to manifest giftings.

He has armed you with basic weapons to use. He is your Commander and is watching over your progress in the battle, and when a gift is needed he will provide it. If no gift comes, then battle on with your basic weapons. Obviously He can see you will win the city with those weapons.

Remember, the majority of cities taken by Joshua were just with swords and spears, their basic weapons.

PRESENT BOOT CAMP

Most Christians have a desire to operate in both levels of weaponry and yet the ability to be fulfilled in these areas seems to be beyond the grasp of many.

Perfection in the use of God's weaponry is not seen overnight. Remember what Joel's army was told: "Prepare War!" I believe within several years, we are going to see multitudes armed with all the weaponry that God wants for them.

God is restoring the church and is restoring the "old" training camp methods.

Right around the world people are not just talking about weapons but instructing the saints in their use and giving them practical opportunities. They are fulfilling the role given to apostles, prophets, evangelists, pastors and teachers to equip the saints for the work of THEIR ministry.

Our own evangelistic ministry which was once a pure thrust for souls in the third world has seen changes. After my experience at the auto auction in Australia, God showed me His plan was to train up an army of people to take their own cities. What better place to train people than in third world countries? Although the physical conditions are certainly more harsh, spiritually it is a lot easier and results of salvation and healing can be more easily attained.

Some nations are spiritually hard and on a spiritual rating from 1 to 10, might rate an 8.

Some of the third world nations are experiencing breakthrough and might rate 2 or 3.

When training anybody on anything, early success is an important factor. Encouraged by the success in those nations, they can return home stronger and see breakthrough in the spiritually tougher places of their own hometowns.

Our trips to third world countries are obviously not just tourist trips to look at and observe third world churches, but are practical boot camps for the training of His army.

This is not some "NEW" training method. We caught the concept from JESUS.

How did He teach His disciples? He demonstrated His works, taught them and released them to do the same thing.

Many pastors, seeing the advantages of training their people through this method, have joined us and now many teams of people under local church leadership are going forward into foreign fields.

We have also commenced Boot Camp Seminars in Western countries for those who have not been able to go on overseas trips. In these, we both teach and give practical experience of both preaching and praying for the sick.

This type of training will spread right throughout the body and will become an accepted way of training over the next few years.

I have heard some preachers refer to "old time" religion where they make reference to a church of holiness.

The **real** old time religion is upon us where the saints will not only move in Godly holiness but in Godly power as well. "Old time" religion of doing the works that Jesus did is making its return and the call to be trained for war is being trumpeted.

God will make available opportunities to be trained. When seminars are held or practical boot camps are on, get to them and learn to release what God has placed in you. Begin to put into practice what your pastors are teaching you.

Remember, placed in you is a stockpile of His power waiting to be used.

Chapter 9

MISUSE OF THE WEAPON OF PRAYER

"What about prayer; surely it is a basic weapon of the church," you may say.

Yes, it is, but we have purposely left this form of attack till now, as many have previously thought that prayer was THE answer.

Paul tells us in Ephesians 6:18 to pray with *"all prayer"*. Another translation says *"different kinds of prayer"*. We must realize that God has different kinds of prayer for different situations. Because of this misunderstanding, many prayers for evangelism have been slightly misdirected.

We have prayed for personal needs like:

"Lord give me wisdom in this situation."

"Lord I need your strengthening right now."

"Lord please meet my daily needs."

And so we thought our prayer for evangelism should go along the same lines.

One typical prayer for the world goes something like this—we kneel beside our beds, put our hands together and pray:

Lord, save them in Africa!

Lord, save them in China!

Lord, save them in India!

Lord, save Uncle Sam, Aunty Flo and
bless Felix our cat.
Amen.

Although, obviously oversimplified, it is a model form by which many expect to move the hand of God.

The basis of the message is telling God to "GO YE". The problem becomes obvious now, because He has already told us that we must be the ones who "GO".

Christ (the head) has given an order to His body (that's us, His arms and legs on the earth) to go and preach and lay hands on the people of the earth.

In response to that, many, not understanding the complete picture, have turned back to our Head and said: "No, you Go!"

In a normal body, if the head were sending a message to the arms to tell it to do something, and the arms were sending the same message back to the head, we'd have a short circuit around the neck. The result? Paralysis!

Paralysis in evangelism has set into the church because of the confusion to many who are supposed to do the "GOING"! Messages go from the Head to us to "GO" and we keep sending the same message back up to Him.

"GO SAVE THEM, GOD!"

Now I am certainly not against prayer, but we must ensure that our prayer is in line with scripture and not misdirected. We have listed three basic types of prayer which may help you in evangelism.

PRAYER No. ONE: EVANGELISM BLUEPRINT

Our Commander has given us a blueprint prayer especially for evangelism and it is found in Matthew 9:37, 38. It immediately puts its finger on the problem.
"THE HARVEST IS TRULY PLENTIFUL"

But what is the basic problem? Do we need to pray for God to move on our behalf? No, it continues:
"THE LABOURERS ARE FEW"

That's the key God is needing—more labourers! Our prayer instruction now follows:

"THEREFORE PRAY THE LORD OF HIS HARVEST THAT HE WILL SEND FORTH LABOURERS INTO HIS HARVEST".

Prayer is needed, but not to be misdirected into commanding God to go. Rather that He will send out labourers. One translation says, pray that He will "thrust out" labourers.

I have a pretty good idea why we need to pray for labourers to be THRUST out. Our model prayer for evangelism should be —
Lord raise and thrust labourers into China!
Lord raise and thrust labourers into India!
Lord raise and thrust labourers into Africa!
Lord thrust somebody out to go and preach the gospel to Aunty Flo and Uncle Sam.

Mark 11:24 says: *"Therefore I say to you, whatever things you ask when you pray, believe that you receive them, and you will have them."*

I find personally that it is much easier to "believe" that a labourer will preach to my Aunt Flo than to believe that I am going to move God somewhere up there near Cloud Nine down to "somehow" touch the one I am praying for.

You need to "believe that you receive".

As much as we are praying for others to be raised and thrust out, realize that all the other Christians have Aunt Flos and Uncle Sams, and other unsaved friends and relatives.

They are praying that somebody like you will share the gospel with them. These unsaved are living next door, they work with you, you meet them in the supermarket or at sporting or social functions. As much as we pray for the unsaved we know, we should be readily available to be the answer for other Christians'prayers and be willing to be thrust out as well.

"DO IT THEMSELVES" METHOD?

But doesn't the Bible say "whosoever shall call upon the name of the Lord shall be saved?" " Surely I could pray for somebody and they could then call out to the Lord." You may think. Yes it does say that in Romans 10:13, but it doesn't end there. In verses 14 and 15 it goes on to say:

1. How shall they call on Him in whom they have not believed?
2. And how shall they believe on Him of whom they have not heard?
3. And how shall they hear without a preacher?
4. And how shall they preach unless they are sent?

God's goal for evangelism involves believers. He has decreed we are to be ones who will share in the joy of bringing in His harvest.

PRAYER No. TWO: THE ATTACKING PRAYER

Assuming now we have our soldiers ready to attack and be thrust out, we have a prayer of warfare for them.

Let us again get a mental picture of the unsaved, a walled city with king satan ruling over them. As their ruler and thought provoker, he is continually feeding them propaganda against God and the church, and continues to influence power over them through this method. 2 Corinthians 4:4 tells us that they are people *"whose mind the god of this age has blinded."*

We are told in Ephesians 6:12 that we are not fighting the unsaved person, but the spiritual ruler over them.

FEAR
DIVORCE
PAIN
BITTERNESS
HURT
REJECTION
STRESS
ANXIETY
GUILT
SHAME
DEPRESSION

This strong ruler influences their lifestyle and his power over them needs to be bound if we are to get the person away from his control.

"No one can enter a strong man's house and plunder his goods, unless he first binds the strong man, and then he will plunder his house." (Mark 3:27)

King satan needs to be bound. How do we do that? Do we ask God to do it?

No!

You have been given power and authority over all the works of the devil and demons. (Luke 10:19).

Jesus has also told us:

"Assuredly, I say to you, whatever you bind on earth will be bound in heaven, and whatever you loose on earth will be loosed in heaven." (Matthew 18:18)

By binding the forces in the Name of Jesus Christ, you restrict the deceitful influence of their present ruler. Our goal is by prayer, to bring the people to a point where they will be able to 'see' and understand the gospel message without their rulers' influence.

So, using a combination of both the weapon of prayer and the gospel we can break through the gates of the city.

IT HASN'T WORKED FOR ME !

Many have professed praying in line with this type of spiritual attack and have met with limited success. Perhaps we then should look very carefully at how we have been praying.

We are told in James 5:16 *"...The effective, fervent prayer of a righteous man avails much."*

If we have not 'availed much', then lets see perhaps where we may have missed it.

"Effective"

First of all, our prayer is to be "effective". How do we make it effective? We are told in Mark 11:24: *"Therefore I say to you, whatever things you ask when you pray, believe that you receive them, and you will have them."*

Your prayer will only be effective if you **believe** in your heart that you've received the answer. Many in the past have prayed and bound spiritual forces way above what they really can have a heart belief for.

They have prayed for the whole church to be filled, entire cities and even nations to be taken. Now if God has placed a burden on you and you have a heart belief in those areas, fine, pray.

But for the majority of us, why not start praying for one, two or maybe three people?

Claim them and begin to bind the forces over their lives. As you meet success with one, two and then a few, faith will rise in your heart to believe for greater numbers.

God already has people for you to reach. Pray and ask wisdom from the Lord as to where you should start. As He gives you the names or faces of people, write their names down and commence a prayer warfare over their lives.

"Fervent"

Nothing brings forward "fervent" prayer like seeing the real plight of the person you have claimed. Remember the love of the parent when the little girl was attacked by that mad dog. Get a picture in your mind of people, each one unhappy in different ways because of the walls of bondage which their present king has inflicted on them. Their king is enjoying every moment of it ravaging them with sickness, disease and hurts.

Let a violent anger rise in your heart toward him and his painful rule.

Remember we are not fighting the person, but "him", the ruler. Your fervent prayer of violence can tear into the spirit realm, binding and restricting him.

Understanding the hurts that are continuously upon them will be a catalyst to see you engage in a continual fight, shaking the forces of darkness over their lives.

The Amplified Bible translation says: "The earnest (heartfelt, continued) prayer makes tremendous power available, dynamic in its working." Pray right now for those people, breaking and binding the influence of the enemy. Your fervent prayer can involve "all kinds" of prayer. Praying in the spirit, and with understanding, will generate tremendous, dynamic power.

Get a faith picture of each one, saved, healed, set free, standing in church with a smile on his or her face, glorifying God. Give the Lord a prayer of praise for the completed victory.

HOW LONG DO I PRAY ?

The question is not how long should I pray, but how much will I pray? How much time is the unsaved person worth? Can you give them one minute a day or an hour a day?

The bible says to *"pray without ceasing"* (1 Thessalonians 5:17). The Amplified says: *"Be unceasing in prayer—praying perserveringly."* If you really plant a picture in your mind of their problems and bondage, that picture will come before your mind, continually motivating you. Pray whenever you can for them, on the way to work, in the lunch hour. Some may get saved quickly, others take time. There are no rules except "Pray perserveringly until you see victory".

PRAYER No. THREE: GUIDANCE

After our attacking the spiritual forces over their lives, there will come the time for a frontal attack, when you need to talk to people and give them the good news.

When Joshua and his men took the city of Ai, God gave him the wisdom and guidance on how to do it. We are told in James 1:5:

"If any of you lacks wisdom, let him ask of God, who gives to all liberally and without reproach, and it will be given to him."

We can ask the Lord what to say and He will give us the right words at the right time.

He told His original Guerrillas what to do when they were brought before kings and rulers.

"Therefore settle it in your hearts not to meditate beforehand on what you will answer; for I will give you a mouth and wisdom which all your adversaries will not be able to contradict or resist." Luke 21:14-15

The promise can be claimed by God's modern day Guerrilla force.

I have found with every person that I have witnessed to, the way and what I discussed were always different. Pray that the Lord will guide your actions and words. That doesn't mean that you go out in ignorance. Learn all about the gospel of the Kingdom and its benefits, and God will guide your use in it.

GOD'S SEASONS

One of the greatest hindrances to further evangelism for many has been the waiting for God's appointed revival time for a nation. Where did this line of thought find its roots?

God through parables and other scriptures, such as found in Matthew 9:37-37; and Matthew 13:36-38, likens the earth to a field, with the people in the world as the wheat, and the saints as the labourers who are to bring in the harvest. This would obviously lead us to reason that grain has to ripen and that reaping could only be achieved in a certain season.

Many have been praying for the rain of the Holy Spirit and the end time harvest to hit their area. With this reasoning, it is obviously senseless for a labourer to try to bring in a harvest out of season, and so a thinking can set in that we simply have to sit back and wait for God and the Holy Spirit to move. Evidences of such great moves of God have been witnessed in different parts of the world. Great outpourings and harvest have been recorded in Nagaland and other parts of the world such as South America and Indonesia.

The Holy Spirit moves sovereignly, even through children, to prophesy, preach and perform healings. The reports come back to us and we simply stand in awe at what God did. It was His season, His timing.

"Oh yes", we say: "that's what we need here, God! Move by your Spirit!"

Now these revival moves seemed to bypass all known principles of evangelism.

Our teaching so far is that it is man, armed with weapons of warfare, who goes out and brings the harvest in.

The weapons have been given to the saints, and God is waiting for them to use them.

God or Man

Now which is it — God pouring out His Spirit, or man advancing?

Both answers are correct. Again, it is easy to explain in line with the Jericho teaching. I believe, in answer to prayer that binds spiritual forces over nations, God can and does move above man's normal abilities and faith levels.

A Jericho takes place over a whole nation, the walls of bondage fall, and everyone stands in awe.

"Nagalands" and the like will continue to happen. However on seeing this great outpouring, an assumption can be formed that this is the way God is going to do it. Prayer goes up in every country expecting a Jericho, a great harvest.

Jesus does not want the church just sitting, waiting and praying for a future harvest.

His disciples were also well aware of timings and seasons, and He rebuked them. He said: *"Do not say, 'There are still four months and then comes the harvest.' Behold, I say to you, lift up your eyes and look at the fields,for they are already white for harvest!"* (John 4:35).

He was saying: "Yes, we do have great outpourings up the road and seasons of harvest, but just don't talk about them. Open up your eyes, you can harvest today. There are souls all around you, individuals who are ripe for the picking."

This "revival is coming" thinking has made spiritual paraplegics out of many potential God's Guerrillas.

God is waiting for you to present yourself for training and then go as a labourer, prepared not only to pray for present and future harvest, but to bring them in as well. Get out of your chair today. Shake the rust off your armour and get oiled up in the Holy Ghost ready for action. Come on you accountants, lawyers, doctors, labourers, housewives, politicians.

"THE FIELDS ARE ALREADY WHITE FOR HARVEST"

UNCLE SAM NEEDS JESUS

Chapter 10

HOME BASE

Our regular gathering of the saints, the church, forms a base from which we can operate our guerrilla strikes. The home base is an integral part of success in the war.

Again the Encyclopaedia Britannica explains:

"Guerrilla forces cannot fight all the time. They must control safe areas to which they can retire voluntarily or involuntarily, for rest, recuperation and repair of arms, clothing and equipment and where recruits can be indoctrinated, trained and equipped."

Your regular weekly meetings are a safe area where you can receive R & R (rest and recuperation), be built up and then return to your next six days of war.

Apart from the offensive weaponry God has given you, he has given you other gifts to help comfort, boost morale and exhort those who may be a little battle weary.

"As each one has received a gift, minister it to one another, as good stewards of the manifold grace of God." (1 Peter 4:10)

This can be operated depending on the varying giftings God has given you. It may be that you are blessed financially and you are able to bless some of the less fortunate troops.

You may possibly have a "helps" ministry and be able to assist in numerous ways. You may invite troops over to your home for dinner and lift and exhort them. Your gifting may be a word of prophecy, tongues, interpretation of tongues or words of personal encouragement.

Our desire to see the war won will motivate us to love, exhort and lift others. The battle is getting hotter and high morale among the troops is paramount. That is why we are commanded to come together at home base. We are told in Hebrews 10:25: *"Not forsaking the assembling of ourselves together, as is the manner of some, but exhorting one another, and so much the more as you see the Day approaching."*

We are in the days when assembling together and exhortation are not an option, they are essential.

THE OFFICERS

For the home base to operate efficiently we must have a chain of command, so there is order and no confusion. Let us list the posts and who fulfills them:

Commander in Chief — Jesus Christ;
Generals, Colonels & other Officers — Apostles, Prophets, Pastors, Evangelists and Teachers;
Enlisted men — The rest of saints of God.

Your home base officers are the full time ministry whose job entails training you for the work of your ministry. (Ephesians 4:11-12)

They are there to give your morale a boost, teach the use of offensive and defensive weapons, teach army obedience, provide tactical training and recuperative help to all those who have been out fighting all week.

They also take charge of all the new converts who have defected from satan's army and indoctrinate and train them so that they might become soldiers like you.

TOP GUNS

Possibly we can now see the role of evangelists and other visiting ministries in a slightly different light. An important aspect of their role is to equip you for the work of your ministry.

We have traditionally seen the role of the evangelist as the "TOP GUN" who is going to blast the town apart for Jesus. He is supposed to stride into town like a spiritual John Wayne with both barrels blazing,

BIG CROWDS ... BIG HEALINGS ... BIG SALVATION !

Many have made heroes of them and thought they were to do it all, while the saints stood back in absolute awe.

The apostle Paul has something to say about that attitude. Paul (a TOP GUN himself) saw his role more than one of being the "spiritual heavy" who blasted the devil's work.

He spoke to the Corinthian Church and told them: *"Be ye followers of me, even as I also am of Christ"* (1 Corinthians 11:1, K.J.V.)

The word for "followers" (mimetes) means to mimic or imitate. Paul was saying to the saints, "Imitate me as I imitate Christ." He imitated Christ in all ways, in boldness, in healing, in preaching, in casting out demons.

He didn't have an attitude that he was supposed to be "THE" ministry while everyone else "the followers" were arm chair spectators.

Unfortunately many saints today have caught onto the word "followers" and that's all they have become. Many have become followers or fans of certain ministries, giving them some super hero status. Many have picked up the traits of a fan that would follow a pop group.

I follow Kenneth !

I follow Billy !

I follow Jimmy !

"This one is best!"

"No, mine is more powerful!"

"Yes, but this one is a better teacher!"

Many are such good "fans", they keep a collection of all their tapes and keep up with all the latest action in magazines.

"Have you read his latest book?"

"Have you seen the recent video?"

Now it's not wrong to look up to great men of God ... but ...

NOT ONE OF THESE MEN OF GOD WANTS YOU TO BECOME HIS FAN OR FOLLOWER

The heart of their ministry, and the reason they put out tapes, books, magazines and videos is **so you can imitate Christ as they are imitating Christ.**

If you see a flaw in a man of God, pray for him Only imitate him in the areas he imitates Christ.

But it is time we stopped just being fans and followers and became doers of the word as they are.

HOW WE "IMITATE"

When evangelists come to town or to our home base, they do draw crowds. In our minds, we think they are huge crowds.

I hear people say with wide eyes: "There were THOUSANDS at the crusade."

Now it's good to have "huge" crowds and to know that the unsaved are hearing the gospel with signs and wonders following. But "huge" in comparison to what?

What about the other 99 per cent of the people in your city who didn't come to the meeting?

Praise God for the anointed ministry of the evangelist.

Yes, we must agree God does have an important ministry for the evangelist, but it's not God's plan to have everyone saved through him. It is great to go, and be excited at these meetings but remember part of his ministry is to help equip you.

God gets these "TOP GUNS" through your town and home base certainly to get people saved, but also to demonstrate the weaponry available to the church.

"But I don't work miracle healings like him," you might say.

Yes, admittedly, he will exhibit more "Jericho" healings than you. This is a gifting God gives him "as the Spirit wills". But remember what Jericho also did for the troops. It was an encouragement to let them know God was really with them.

God is saying to us through these men: "Hey look, I really am the same yesterday, today and forever. My promise of healing is available!"

When we see "Jericho" healings, let us lift up ourselves again in faith, realizing that with our rifles and grenades we can go and do like the old testament army, take cities with our basic weapons.

When the anointed evangelist comes, listen carefully to his message, take notes and see if you can implement some of his words into sharpening the sword in your mouth. See him healing the sick and get a confirmation in your heart and picture yourself doing the same thing out on the field of battle.

Remember, he has not come to put on a show for you, but to train you. Make every school lesson count.

FIGHTING ON THE BASE ?

Traditional thinking has sometimes stopped the home base being used for its original intentions.

Can you imagine a soldier inviting the enemy back to his training camp? Can you picture him saying: "Please come, I've got something back there I'm sure you'd be very interested in."

Do you think the other side may be a "little" suspicious.

There is no way they'd go back there; they'd realize they'd be walking into an ambush and be blasted.

We must realize the majority of people in your community do not want and will not go to your "home base". Do you think they are stupid? When you pleadingly invite them to come to your church, they know exactly what will happen to them; it means they will get a blast from some "BIG SHOT".

People are generally very nervous about our "BIG SHOTS". Don't you realize what usually happens in a group of unsaved people when you bring in a minister or other "TOP GUNS"? Immediately the cities feel under siege—the gates slam and the shutters are pulled down.

Why do you insist on inviting people to the only place in town where they don't want to go?

This is why God wants His Guerrillas out in the community to touch the 90 percent plus. With no uniform you can walk up and begin talking without getting their guard up before you even start. This is what God wants, His out-of-uniform soldiers going out into the workplace, supermarkets, sporting clubs, social groups getting them saved and healed. Get those who were once "enemies" of God to defect to the new army and bring them back to home base for indoctrination and recruitment training.

This is how the early church acted. They went to the religious and others. *"And daily in the temple, and in every house, they did not cease teaching and preaching JESUS AS THE CHRIST".* (Acts 5:42)

Use your home as a small outpost from which you continue guerrilla strikes during the six days a week of attack.

Chapter 11

BACK STABBING

The home base (the church) as we said, is a controlled safe area for the troops to withdraw and be refreshed.

Unfortunately, the devil knows the importance of morale, and can use those within our own camp to destroy and divide by in-fighting.

Everyone should be involved in the war effort, but some not wishing to get involved in any fighting can become arm chair critics and want to tell everyone else what they are doing wrong. Many forget their correct ministry of fighting and then exhorting and now as a result of their unfulfilment have begun shooting other soldiers with criticism.

"Death and life are in the power of the tongue." (Proverbs 18:21)

In some churches the officers have had to spend the majority of the time doctoring and giving surgery to Guerrillas who have received stab wounds inflicted by those supposedly on the same side.

The end result is that the intended attacking headquarters is transformed into a base hospital.

In fact, if there are minor wounds these should be attended to by the other Guerrillas and pass onto the medical corp the more serious cases. This gives the commanding officers time to plan, direct, and change the new converts into seasoned troops.

MURMURING — THE DEADLY WEAPON

One of the greatest hindrances to the blessings in the home base is that of the complaining soldier. When Joshua did take Jericho, the army was instructed to march around the city for seven days.

Now Joshua had commanded the people saying: *"You shall not shout or make any noise with your voice, nor shall any word proceed out of your mouth, until the day I say to you, 'Shout!'* (Joshua 6:10)

The army was not allowed to say a word. Why?

God had given the leader a vision. Sometimes the army can't see all that God has given a particular officer. But He gives the army a role to play to fulfill that particular goal or vision. Sometimes even the leader can't see **all** the reasons why God is asking them to do a particular task. Many times our actions are one piece of a gigantic jigsaw puzzle. Our Commander in Chief, Jesus, sees the total picture, and as we play our part and fit into His plans, the whole purpose will eventually be plain to see.

If Joshua's army was allowed to talk, it wouldn't be too long before dissension would take place.

"No one's ever taken a city this way before."

"Joshua has been looking a little strange lately."

"I think Caleb would have made a better leader. I'm sure he wouldn't have us doing dumb things like this."

After a few days of complaining, grumbling and murmuring there would have been total division in the camps. Some for Joshua, some against and the army would have been split.

That's why God said: "Nor shall any word proceed out of your mouth."

Just be obedient. Don't question it.

Obedience had its reward — the walls crashed, a mighty victory achieved.

We wonder today why we don't achieve great victories and I believe whole heartedy that murmuring and grumbling are a great cause. It is one of satan's favourite subversive tactics. We are told in Exodus 14:14 NAS:

"The Lord will fight for you; you need only to be silent."

If you want to open your mouth in the middle of a battle, praise Him.

Actually, Moses had the same problem of murmuring under his rule. The people thought that Moses had gone crazy and they'd be better off back in Egypt. Listen to the revelation that Moses comes up with about murmuring:

"...For the Lord hears your murmurings which you make against Him. And what are we? Your murmurings are not against us but against the Lord." (Exodus 16:8)

They thought they were complaining about Moses, but Moses was only God's ambassador. They weren't murmuring against Moses but against God Himself.

PEACE PEOPLE ... MURMURERS

And let us once again remind you of how they got themselves in this horrible situation. They chose not to go to war as the Lord had told them. They wanted peace.

Our picture here shows us that "peaceful" churches that don't go to war will start to grumble among themselves and murmur against their leader. They are stuck in the middle in the desert. Not really wishing to go back and not having either direction or faith (or both) to go forward. Bible history records they will die in the desert.

This can apply to people, individual churches and whole denominations.

Don't get angry with me; if the cap fits, wear it. If you are in the desert, God is sounding an alarm for you to "WAKE UP" and move forward to war.

In relating the story of Moses in 1 Corinthians 10:11 it tells us: *"Now all these things happened to them as examples, and they were written for our admonition, on whom the ends of the ages have come."*

A list of all the reasons they died are found in verses 7-10:

1. Idolatry
2. Sexual immorality
3. Tempting Christ
4. Murmuring

When I read "murmuring" in there with all those other hideous sins, I thought I must have misread it.

"They died because of murmuring? Surely not!" I thought.

I mean, it seemed to stick out like a sore toe. It was like, pick the wrong one in the group — gold, silver, diamonds, rubbish bin.

Surely a little grumble here or there isn't going to hurt much. Surely God can't look on murmuring as badly as idolatry.

The truth is "THEY DIED BECAUSE OF IT"; and this is a lesson to us to whom the end of the ages has come.

Why does God look upon it so strongly? Leaders are God's ambassadors. When you murmur against them, you murmur directly against God.

I just wonder how many potential ministries have died because of murmuring. How many people wondering why they haven't been used. Oh yes, they are physically alive, but their spiritual use to God has been buried.

BUT ... MY OFFICERS

"But you don't know my officers—there is plenty to murmur at! I find it hard to submit myself to them," you may be thinking.

IF YOU CAN'T SUBMIT TO YOUR OFFICER, PRAY ABOUT IT AND LET GOD LEAD YOU TO A CHURCH WHERE YOU CAN OBEY.

"But brother, I know God has called me to the church I'm at now."

THEN BE OBEDIENT TO THE OFFICER GOD HAS PLACED YOU UNDER. HE'S PUT YOU THERE TO LEARN SOMETHING.

"Likewise, you younger people, submit yourselves to your elders. Yes, all of you be submissive to one another, and be clothed with humility, for God resists the proud, but gives grace to the humble." (1 Peter 5:5)

Remember again, murmuring against His leadership is murmuring against God. If you see flaws in your officers, pray for them. Only imitate them in the areas which they are imitating Christ.

The sooner you start to realize that there are no perfect churches, officers or soldiers, the sooner you may stop grumbling and get on with the job of changing yourself into the image of Christ and doing His works.

Chapter 12

"HOME BASE" NON-COMBATANTS

As we have previously discussed, many Guerrillas have thought their ministry was centred around home base.

Somehow the idea has crept into some minds that the defeating of the devil's brigade could be done back at the home base through the weapon of PRAISE. Like "PRAYERS" many "PRAISERS" have thought that they have THE answer to devil defeating.

The thinking arises after reading the exciting story of Jehoshaphat's army in 2 Chronicles 20 when they were faced with opposition from the Amorites and Moabites.

Although they were overwhelmingly outnumbered and outgunned, the Lord, their Commanding Officer, was keeping an overall view of the situation. Acknowledging the apparent hopelessness of the situation, they prayed for guidance.

"*... For we have no power against this great multitude that is coming against us, nor do we know what to do, but our eyes are upon You.*" (2 Chronicles 20:12)

He gave them a type of tactic that had never been used before. The singers were to be placed up the front of the army and sing praises to God as they led the army down towards the enemy.

As they did this, the Lord used His spiritual artillery to fire rounds of confusion into the opposition's camp. The Amorites and Moabites ambushed each other and Jehoshaphat's army marched in and took the spoils of battle without even raising a sword.

Obviously we see another type of "Jericho" situation here—the Commander- in-Chief assessing the situation and helping His troops with additional spiritual weaponry. This again was not the normal way God conducted His battles, but as with Joshua, as they were obedient to His orders, He moved on their behalf.

By reading this story by itself, and not understanding the overall war picture we can make the same mistake as with prayer, and think that praise is THE answer.

MUSICAL TALENTS

Some Guerrillas with musical talents after being taught on this story have suddenly seen "their ministry".

They are to be "up front" leading the army! Unfortunately because they don't understand their full role, the "up front" seems to be for most, standing in full view of the church on Sundays, as the choir, individual singers or band.

Because they now have "their ministry", they have been given special status above the other troops and seek exemption from the battle during the week and become non-combatants.

Unfortunately, because they only got a part of the picture, they are missing out on the most exciting part of their ministry—preaching, healing and destroying the devil's works.

Let's try to correct the picture so that they can be released.

First of all, the singers in Jehoshaphat's army weren't taking place in a church service, they were out front leading the army toward the enemy. "Tomorrow, go down against them", was the order given.

Now they knew the Lord was going to move on their behalf, but they still had to march out towards the enemy, being obedient and being prepared to even die.

It wasn't till after they had moved out, that they saw how God's plan was going to work.

If we wish to take that picture for today's army, then those musically talented should be "up front" leading the rest of the church into the enemy's territory in evangelism.

WRONG PICTURE

As we discussed, we cannot exactly use the examples of God's old testament army for today. God's Guerrillas are a completely different kind of spiritual force. In the old testament there were different offices given!

God anointed kings, priests, and they also had singers!

"Who are the priests today?" We are!

"Who are the kings today?" We are!

"Who are the praisers today?" We are!

(Rev 1:6; Heb 13:15; Eph 5:19)

God doesn't even differentiate between races or sexes, He sees neither Greek nor Jew, male nor female. (Galatians 3:28)

This guerrilla army is made up of "believers."

All believers can praise God for the victory as we march off, by ourselves, or in small guerrilla units, into the neighbour's house, supermarket or offices.

We obviously don't need a special group of singers going before us. Can you imagine going and witnessing to your neighbour to the accompaniment of a band?

How many singers went before the apostle Paul as he went out to do battle? Can you picture him in prison, sending off a telegram to Peter and John:

"SEND DOWN THE CHURCH CHOIR, I NEED TO GET OUT OF HERE!"

No! As he praised God he was released. He was the praiser, priest and king. Paul tells us in 1 Corinthians 4:16: *"Therefore I urge you, imitate me."*

In God's Guerrillas everyone is to go to war, being God's praiser, priest and king.

"Well what about the musically talented?" You may ask: "Do they just forget about their ministry in music ?"

Definitely not!

As well as being front line fighters, they can be exhorters, encouragers and morale boosters,in song both at home base on Sundays and on the battle field during the week.

We praise God for those Guerrilla musicians who have come on our crusades, preached, healed and cast out demons, alongside the other Guerrillas and then exhorted and boosted us with their song.

Other musicians who have studied the gospel of the kingdom and incorporated the message into song have directly preached through their music and seen the devil's works destroyed. I may add that the songs had effect because it was the gospel and not just "entertaining" music.

COLLECTING THE SPOILS

Even though we may grasp the picture that every Guerrilla is to be a praiser, a lingering thought may come in that all we still have to do is praise, and God does the rest.

In the story of Jehoshaphat's army, we must realize that even after their praising, the task was still not complete.

"When Jehoshaphat and his people came down to take away their spoil, they found among them an abundance of valuables in the dead bodies ..." (2 Chronicles 20:25)

After praise they had the reward of collecting the valuables and spoils of battle. I am sure, the singers, like the rest of the army, thoroughly enjoyed emptying out the pockets of the enemy.

What are valuables and spoils today?

People are the spoil ..... The unsaved who are so valuable to us and to our Commander. They are presently, however, in the pocket of satan.

Our praise can be a weapon of warfare to destroy the devil's control and stonghold over their lives.

Used in conjunction with prayer, it can deaden the spiritual forces around them, and so we can go in and clean out satan's pockets.

How do we do that?

How do we reach out and collect the spoils of victory today? We reach out through the preaching of the gospel! We have found on many occasions after a combination of prayer and praise, those witnessed to were "easy pickings."

Some actually have come to us asking questions about the Lord. No fight, no opposition, every pocket of resistance was opened up.

Sometimes the battles are easy like this, other times more weaponry is needed. We need to remember like Joshua, there are no two cities the same. Some are easier, some harder, and both wisdom and guidance are needed for each attack.

OTHER NON-COMBATANTS

We can begin to see that whether it be in the use of basic weapons, gifts, prayer or praise, Jesus wants us all to be involved in the joy of going into all the world, preaching to everyone, and experiencing, the reward of bringing back the spoils of victory.

Every believer has a DUAL ministry, firstly one of love and exhortation towards other saints but also another ministry to reconcile the unsaved to God.

"Now all things are of God who has reconciled us to Himself through Jesus Christ, and HAS GIVEN US THE MINISTRY OF RECONCILIATION;" (2 Corinthians 5:18)

Unfortunately, many others in the church have also missed out in the excitement of the war because they thought "their ministry" was only behind the lines.

Some have been used to give words of direction and encouragement, others have shared visions and still others have been intercessors. Many of them, not understanding God's purposes for all believers, have not entered the war zone themselves.

We have some good news for you. You are Guerrillas as well!

Praise God for your present exhorting and strengthening ministry, but you too, like the singers, have a place in the battle field, bringing in the "valuables" and sharing in the rewards of victory.

Chapter 13

CONVENTIONAL OR GUERRILLA WAR?

"But surely," you may say, "even in a conventional army, not everyone is a front line soldier."

There is normally only a relatively small force at the front directly engaging the enemy, with a much larger non-combatant, "back up" force who keep them on the field."

I could not agree more wholeheartedly ... If I were talking about a conventional army!

Let's look at the large gulf of discrepancies that sets our army apart from the traditional one by firstly conducting a review of the supply and "back up" services.

1.	Weapons	These are supplied free of charge by the Holy Spirit.
2.	Food	You do not march down to the mess and line up for "army" food. You provide your own.
3.	Accommodation	No long army barracks here. You supply your own or you may be assisted by other Guerrillas.
4.	Uniforms	No army issue.
5.	Finance	Your daily job provides the money to finance your Guerrilla ministry and help

others. You sub-contract other companies and people in the world, to provide food, accommodation, clothing and all other needs to keep you on the field.

Your tithes and offerings are given through your home base to your Commander in Chief, Jesus, for a central fighting fund. Out of this, He finances the officers, maintains your home base and helps establish further bases.

This unique system dispenses with the need for many of the conventional army non combatant roles. Office workers, kitchen staff, builders, payroll clerks, need no longer to be filled by full time soldiers who do not fight.

Without this huge drain on soldiers, it makes for a lean, mean fighting machine.

It releases a majority to fight instead of a minority, and it gives each Guerrilla a mixture of secular work and combat, so giving his or her life the variety and excitement that we all need.

This system also allows for maximum infiltration into enemy territory.

NEHEMIAH'S GUERRILLAS

It is easy to demonstrate further differences between conventional and guerrilla warfare.

Conventional warfare takes place when two countries, each with clearly defined territorial lines, fight one another. The two line their forces up against the opposing side and try to force the other back.

Is there any country in the world that Christians totally control?

Our picture of warfare today is not the conventional one of satan's troops lined up on one side and Jesus' troops lined up on the other, with both armies backed up fully from the rear. Today it is unconventional guerrilla warfare.

In the old testament, Nehemiah found himself having to fight this unconventional type of warfare, and perhaps we can learn some principles from his experience.

In Nehemiah's time, God's people had been overrun by the enemy and they controlled no territory at all, but he had been ordered by God to counter- attack by rebuilding Jerusalem.

The people that helped him were not a gigantic army marching across the land, but a minority group of everyday citizens.

As they began to rebuild the walls, the enemy rose up against them, and as there was no formal army, everyone had to be directly involved in the fighting.

Nehemiah tells us how they fought:

"Therefore I positioned men behind the lower parts of the wall at the openings; and I set the people according to their families, with their swords, their spears and their bows." (Nehemiah 4:13)

Everyone was armed, because the enemy was all around them and they were virtually fighting the war in their own back yard.

Today's unconventional guerrilla army is faced with a similar situation.

Jesus entered into the earth realm to begin rebuilding His Jerusalem, the church. (1Peter 2:5). Like Nehemiah, He entered into occupied enemy territory and was completely surrounded by the devil's works. He was in a similar situation to that of a paratrooper being dropped behind enemy lines on a mission.

Jesus' mission was to fight outwards with guerrilla style fighting, building up His rulership over people's lives, and training up a guerrilla force to continue that mission.

IT WAS NOT CONVENTIONAL!

IT WAS GUERRILLA WARFARE!

The mission is far from complete at this point. Christians today are temporarily an unconventional army and minority force living behind enemy lines. Satan is called the "god of this age" and he is presently the ruler over the vast majority of people. He rules over people who are your neighbours, fellow workers, shoppers and social contacts. You are surrounded by sickness, disease, depression and bad news, through press, radio and television. Your homes are "Good News" guerrilla outposts in the midst of hostile territory.

The war front is not only thousands of kilometres away in India or Outer Mongolia; we are also fighting the war from our own back yard.

When you leave from your outpost you walk into the war zone. God wants the modern army to be motivated like Nehemiah's group. They were told: "... *Fight for your brethren, your sons, your daughters, your wives and your houses.*" (Verse 14)

God wants you trained in the weapons of warfare so you can defend your own outpost and all those you love.

DUAL MINISTRY

We are constantly reminded that although the building of Jerusalem was important there was always the need to be ready to go onto the attack.

"Those who built on the wall and those who carried burdens, loaded themselves so that with one hand they worked at construction and with the other, held a weapon." Everyone of the builders had his sword girded at his side as he built ...." (Verses 17 and 18)

You may, on one hand, have a ministry to build and exhort others. On the other hand you need to be able to wield the sword of the Spirit and be able to go out to battle.

Our Commander Jesus wants training in the use of weaponry for all Guerrillas and new recruits to be able to protect yourselves, fellow soldiers, family and keep the enemy from your outpost.

You will then be expected to conduct small scale attacks into the enemy territory surrounding your camp and extend kingdom domain.

Satan is only the god of this age. There is a new age coming up. We may be a minority, but God wants us to be a majority.

This is why He wants to train all believers to do His works. This is why He has ordered all believers to preach to every creature and for signs and wonders to follow us.

He did not say all believers except for intercessors, visionaries, those who prophesy, singers, musicians, etc, etc, etc. The good news for the "builders" is you get to be trained and fight too.

When do we get to put our sword down?
When all Jesus' enemies are defeated!

FEAR

One of the greatest hindrances to getting those non combatants out of the comfort of home base is fear. The same problem beset the old testament army, and God had a solution for them.

In our principles of war chapter, Deuteronomy 20, we have one solution to this dilemma:

"Then the officers shall speak further to the people, and say, 'What man is there who is fearful and fainthearted. Let him go and return to his house, lest the heart of his brethren faint like his heart.'" (Verse 8)

Our Commanding Officer will not force you to go out and fight if you do not want to. If you are afraid, your fear will be contagious and other Guerrillas will lose heart.

You can get out of fighting the battle a very simple way.

You don't have to flunk the physical.

You don't have to be a conscientious objector.

You don't have to say: "That's not my ministry".

You just have to say: "I'm afraid."

I'm sorry to say that many have hidden behind the "other ministry" excuse. If you do not want to fight, fine, but don't pollute the minds of others who may try to imitate you instead of imitating Christ and doing His works.

"That's a bit tough!" you may think.

No, it's the truth. I'm believing that the truth will set people free from their self imposed limitations and release them to do the works of Jesus.

After all, it was Jesus, not me who said: "He that believe on me, the works that I do shall he do also."

The Lord spoke to me very clearly through a prophetic word, when I was preparing this book:

"LET THERE BE A CLEAR CALL TO WAR!"

That means to spell it out, so everyone clearly understands. Fellow Guerrillas, we are not living in "nice" times. The devil's works are flooding in and unless the standard of the "mighty men" is raised, we will be immersed.

Through Christ's sacrifice at Calvary, all power and authority was given to us. The devil and demons already know it. Jesus wants
YOU to know it!
YOU to be trained!
YOU to go to war!

God's alarm clock is ringing and saying "WAKE UP!"

Clearly, in this time, there are going to be two groups of people: those who, even though they are weak in themselves, are going to trust the Lord and say: "I am strong in Him". And secondly, those who will not believe Him, and settle for peaceful co-existence.

I am not trying to condemn those who choose peaceful co-existence, but rather ensure that the fear and peace mentality does not spread and affect others.

TRAINING REMOVES FEAR

Personally, I believe that the vast majority of people, the intercessors, exhorters, singers and musicians, all Christians, love their Lord and want to go out and fight for Him.

Possibly the main reason they have been afraid to go out stems from past failures. The reason for this, as we have mentioned before, is that they don't know how to use their weapons to the fullest. After failing, they have thought: "That's not for me" and sought another ministry.

Remember again, mighty men, it's "PREPARE WAR" time. Some of the army are trained and others are in the training process. Apart from the ministry you have now, seek out and get teaching and experience, learning and practising the weapons of warfare by witnessing and praying for others under supervised leadership.

You will then be a person who not only keeps sickness, disease and all other enemies from your own home, but you will be a force in seeing the devil's works destroyed in the enemy territory surrounding you.

Chapter 14

COMBINING THE WEAPONS

You now have at your disposal a powerful group of weapons to go and take the unsaved, our spiritual cities. Let's take an agenda of what we have so far. They come in four basic groupings.

GROUP I	Your basic weapons preaching, healing, casting out demons.
GROUP II	Your extra firepower; gifts of the Spirit.
GROUP III	Your prayer power; thrusting, attacking and guiding.
GROUP IV	Praise.

The various combinations of all these weapons are to ensure "the gates of hell will be powerless against us".

God can and does, as we have discussed, move in various ways. But in normal warfare, if not guided in any other method, then we have basic steps which can be taken. As we mentioned earlier, God's Guerrillas' tactics are based on proven methods of warfare used in the old testament. The best and easiest way to take any city is to have the city surrender, open its gates and allow the opposing army to march in.

God reveals wonderful principles for taking cities in Deuteronomy 20 and these keys will enable us to open the gates of hell which are protecting the devil's works.

PRINCIPLE NO. ONE

"When you near a city to fight against it, then proclaim an offer of peace to it." (Deuteronomy 20:10).

Can you picture hundreds of years ago a compassionate king who hears reports of the horrible treatment that an evil neighbouring king is inflicting on his subjects. The good hearted king would be outraged and want to release those subjects from that rule of terror.

I can picture the good king's army singing songs of victory and marching up to a hill near the city. A soldier would then be sent up on horseback under a flag of truce to give them a chance to surrender before the attack began.

We are to see our spiritual cities in the same light. Their lives are a mess at the moment because of their present king.

We are to go up to them, praising God as we go, and knock on the gates of their hearts with the gospel of peace.

We can give them the good news which could be something like this:

"Your lifestyle is horrific because of your present leader, but if you surrender and make Jesus, King, then under His rule you can lead a new lifestyle that will give you righteousness, peace and joy. Open up the gates of your heart and allow God's army of power to march into your city and destroy the works of the devil in your life."

"Mmm," they may say.

"It seems alright, but how do I know that you're telling the truth?"

You may choose to witness of what your life is like under King Jesus, but you also may feel led to give them a sample of Jesus' rulership.

"Look, I notice you are in pain there in your leg. I am going to give you a peace offering of healing as a demonstration of the reality of my King's compassionate power."

"Hey," the person exclaims. "The pain is gone!"

"Now, knowing what kind of King He is, are you willing to surrender your whole city?"

After our gospel message and signs and wonders confirming our word, you may find people react in three different ways:

1. "Yes, I thank you for the peace offering and I surrender my whole city peacefully."
2. "Yes, thanks for the peace offering, but please, no new ruler!" (nine of the 10 lepers healed by Jesus were in this category.)
3. "I don't want any of your message or your offerings. You and your ruler can go and get lost."

PRINCIPLE NO. TWO

What do we do if they do not surrender? Our instruction goes on in verse 12:

"Now if the city will not make peace with you, but would make war against you, then you shall besiege it."

A city can be attacked in many ways. Sometimes instead of wasting manpower and weaponry by storming it, the army would simply surround the city and cut off any supplies of sustenance going in. This method was called sieging and the tactic resulted in bringing the city to its knees.

The attacking king would possibly send up a message from time to time and inquire as to whether they had had enough. This is where our principle of prayer comes in.

"I will encamp against you all around, I will lay siege against you with a mound, and I will raise siegeworks against you." (Isaiah 29:3).

We can raise siegeworks against the city. This is where we release our prayer of binding and loosing and speak in all kinds of prayer. We send, with continued prayer, a barrage of Holy Ghost power into the ruler of that city so he looses control and influence over that person. Perhaps combine it with occasional visits to that city under guidance from your leader to see if they have reconsidered, once again praising God as you go.

We have discovered quite often that as we pray and provide a siegework attack against their leader, satan, it gives him a spiritual migraine. This sends him into confusion and a rage and quite stupidly he begins to take his misery out on his subjects, and makes their lives even more intolerable.

Quite often prayer brings about dramatic changes of circumstances in their lives and they are brought to a point of submission. They are brought to their spiritual knees and surrender their city.

It's not all prayer. It's not all banging at the gates. Each city is different and you will find different combinations of both will be required.

HOW LONG WILL IT TAKE ?

Sometimes when sieging cities, the citizens would surrender immediately. Other times the siege could go on for months or even longer. Our prayer siege and knocking will vary from person to person and in each case we need to be led by the Spirit in the length of our siege. Sometimes we have claimed someone, begun praying and the Lord has led someone else to them and been able to break through the doors. There will be countless combinations of the ways they will be taken.

PAUL'S CONVERSION

We must be very aware that each city or person is different and that God can use so many different ways of reaching each city. Sometimes (as we have previously discussed) when the gospel of peace has not worked, He will send a direct attack of gifts. Through a word of knowledge or gift of healing God will blast a block of bondage off their wall or use some circumstance to get their attention.

This is the type of action that Paul went through. Some praying people mistakenly have thought: "What about Paul? He didn't have the gospel preached to him. God just knocked him off his horse. That's what I'm praying for hard for old Uncle Jack; that God will just hit him like a lightning bolt."

Firstly realize that Paul did hear the gospel preached. Paul, then Saul, was present at the stoning of Stephen and certainly heard, but at that time being blinded by the god of this age, rejected the message.

Now I'm sure the saints put in effective fervent prayer on this man and in this case God by-passed other spiritual weaponry and knocked Paul down. Again I see this as another "Jericho" operation. After a little "wall blasting" he was then in a mind to be able to hear clearly. After his "blast", this was the result. "So he, trembling and astonished, said, 'Lord, what do you want me to do'?"

"Yes, Yes, that's what I'm believing for Uncle Jack! I want God to really knock some sense into him."

Again we ask, how many others received dramatic conversions like Paul's? There is only one recorded. God does answer from time to time like this (as He wills), and we see and hear dramatic conversions. But if we are expecting everyone to be saved by the Jericho—Paul method, you may be very disappointed. Instead, God has asked us to thrust forth labourers armed with an assortment of weapons including prayer to see the rest of the multitudes hear the message.

Chapter 15

I WANT TO BE A "TOP GUN"

We have taught many Indian nationals at our Leadership College at Faith Centre in Hyderabad and have taken over 1,000 people to Third World countries and trained them in practical God's Guerrilla warfare. Many have quickly learnt to shoot spiritual rifles and throw their holy hand grenades. A few,after seeing results of healing and deliverance through their own hands, have thought they should be promoted to be a "TOP GUN" and enter full time service.

Many in the body of Christ, like our team members, have thought that once they begin to use basic weapons or some gifting that they are ready to become an officer. Firstly, let's make a very important point.

JUST BECAUSE YOU CAN SHOOT A RIFLE DOESN'T AUTOMATICALLY MAKE YOU A GENERAL.

As admirable and genuine as their hearts may be to serve the Lord, we must understand about promotion to officer level.

In God's army, *"promotion comes neither from the east nor from the west nor from the south. But God is the Judge."* (Psalm 75:6)

This means you can't go to other soldiers or the officers saying: "Hey, look at me, I'm a great little fighter! How about a lift in the rankings?"

Quite clearly, in reference to the officer rankings it says: *"And He Himself gave some to be apostles, some prophets, some evangelists, and some pastors and teachers."* (Ephesians 4:11)

He, Jesus, is the one who picks the soldiers whom He will promote to lead and train His army. Notice it does not include everyone — He only gave "some". Obviously not everyone can be a leader, otherwise it would be the old story of too many commander in chiefs and not enough indians. He needs the majority of the businessmen, housewives, public servants, doctors and other Guerrillas to be on the field among the unsaved every day.

POWER OR RESPONSIBILITY?

Some privates have thought it must be great to be an officer and be able to give orders to everyone. Let's ensure our motivation for full-time work is correct. Why do you want to become an officer?

TO ORDER OTHERS or TO SERVE OTHERS?

"...But whoever desires to become great among you shall be your servant. and whoever of you desires to be first shall be slave of all." (Mark 10:43,44)

When you become an officer, it means responsibility. Not only responsibility towards others to care and train them, but a responsibility towards God.

"Don't aim at adding to the number of teachers I beg you! Remember that we who are teachers will be judged by a much higher standard." (James 3:1 J.B. Phillips)

If God has called you to be a front line Guerrilla and you self promote yourself, you will find the pressures and responsibility of leadership crushing. It requires Jesus' gift on your life to be successful. Many have crashed in and out of the ministry because of self promotion.

No doubt in this day God is restoring and raising apostles, prophets, pastors, teachers and evangelists, but if Jesus has gifted you the ministry gift will be obvious both to soldiers and officers alike.

"A man's gift makes room for him, and brings him before great men." (Proverbs 18:16)

The problem with many budding officers is that they think they are ready ... NOW. I personally found I had to do a few years apprenticeship as a private before I was promoted to an officer's post.

"Don't cherish exaggerated ideas of yourself or your importance, but try to have a sane estimate of your capabilities." (Romans 12:3 J.B. Phillips)

God may have put you under an officer where you are expected to do perhaps boring and menial tasks. But that is exactly like:

Get in line!

March up and down!

Do 50 push ups!

It's boot camp time and God is seeing if you can be obedient in the small things. Each great man of God did his apprenticeship, boot camp time, under another officer.

Elijah had Elisha, Saul had David, Jesus had his 12, and Paul had his Timothy.

"GOMER PYLE" MENTALITY

I remember, teacher Bob Mumford once mentioning the need to have a Gomer Pyle mentality. For those who may not have heard of him, Gomer was a TV character. A private in the army, he was in love with life and loved any task that he was ordered to do.

His sergeant, who couldn't understand this attitude, was continually infuriated and constantly gave him the most menial tasks.

"Pyle, scrub those garbage bins!" he would order.

"Gol..ll..ee, Sergeant," he would reply.

"I just love scrubbing those rubbish bins. If it will help the army, I'd be thrilled to. Rubbish bin cleaning is one of the greatest jobs there is. I get so fulfilled when I'm cleaning garbage out."

Can we catch the same simplistic attitude and be like little children, enjoying the menial tasks that the sergeants and officers may ask us to do?

We realise that it's for the army war effort and our Commanding Officer:

"... With good will doing service, as to the Lord, and not to men, knowing that whatever good anyone does, he will receive the same from the Lord." (Ephesians 6:7, 8)

God rewards humility and good service towards Him.

"Therefore humble yourselves under the mighty hand of God, that He may exalt you in due time, casting all your care upon Him, for He cares for you." (1 Peter 5:6,7)

Many of us can get anxious and try to get ahead of God. Remember, if you really have a calling, the gift will make room for you and when God is ready to promote you, He'll open a door which nobody can shut. He will promote you at the proper time. In the meantime, keep a humble attitude and cast all your concerns and worries upon Him.

BE A GREAT GUERRILLA!

Others, even though they realize their present position as an enlisted soldier, have thought they should be getting more recognition from the officers because of the ministry they are presently performing. Many feel they should be speaking from the pulpit and telling the other soldiers a thing or too. First of all let's again look at your heart attitude. Do you want to extend "your ministry", or do you want to extend Gods Kingdom? I'm sure that you really want to achieve the latter.

If you really want to encourage the other soldiers, then take note of something an old farmer once told me:

"SHOWIN' IS BETTER THAN TELLIN'."

Go out and do "your ministry" as a soldier, preach the gospel and heal the sick. You need to realize you don't need a pulpit to do your ministry and perform your duty for God. You do your part and let the officers do their part of encouraging, directing, disciplining and training.

The great news for the majority of the army is that they have the exciting task of taking cities. They get to go out on a daily basis destroying the devil's works. If you want to be a "TOP GUN", then aim at being the best crack shot in your platoon. Improve every week, sharpening the weapons of your warfare.

Your preaching and witnessing will get crisper. The numbers captured, saved and healed will increase.

Every week you can march into church bringing in the spoils of battle, a string of new recruits ready to put under your pastor for retraining.

Start at this level — be a good soldier, and do the service as unto the Lord. If you show the Lord your heart is for the Kingdom, not with just lip service but by action, then perhaps you may start to receive recognition from the officers.

Whether they recognise it or not is unimportant — you are doing it for Jesus.

"Servants, be obedient to those who are your masters according to the flesh, with fear and trembling,in sincerity of heart, as to Christ; not with eye service, as men-pleasers, but as servants of Christ, doing the will of God from the heart." (Ephesians 6:5,6)

I know, however, that any pastor would certainly be noticing somebody bringing in new converts every week. Perhaps after becoming the best in the platoon you may receive corporal's or sergeant's stripes, and you will be given the chance to take others out on the field with you to train and to equip.

Let Mark 16:20 be a report of your ministry that will begin this day. Put your name in the spaces provided and read about yourself.

"And .... went out and preached everywhere, the Lord working with .... and confirming the word through the accompanying signs.

Chapter 16

WORRIER OR WARRIOR?

We live in exciting times. All around the world the devil is flooding in his works. Wars, rumours of wars, famines, diseases, terrorist activities and economic instability. The devil is using the tactic of terrorizing the whole earth, and many of the Guerrillas can be caught up in this fear if they aren't careful.

We must again emphasize that he is a counterfeiter and that all his terrorizing and terrorist activities must be a copy. If they are counterfeits, then who are the real terrorists ?

When Joshua's spies went to Jericho to assess the situation, one of the citizens, a woman called Rahab, told them:

"I know that the Lord has given you the land, that the terror of you has fallen on us, and that all the inhabitants of the land are faint-hearted because of you." (Joshua 2:9)

God's old testament army was made up of terrorists.

Today, new testament Guerrilla forces are terrorists who put fear and trembling into the hearts of the army of demonic forces opposing us.

In tactics of terror, the idea is to put so much fear into the opposition that he loses the heart to fight.

There is only one winner. He will terrorize us or we will terrorize him. Satan realizes the link to be broken is your belief, confession and action on God's Word. God, realizing this, gives us strong words, knowing the importance of our continued trust in Him.

He says through Paul:

"...Not in any way terrified by your adversaries..." (Philippians 1:28)

If he can get you fearful and terrorized, you will forget your God. If, on the other hand, you refuse to listen to circumstances, and stand only on what God says, you will reduce him to a terrorized, defeated foe.

Note that Paul tells us, not to be in **any** way terrified.

There are many ways that he can try to terrorize you, and we will be listing now some of those methods. In all cases, though, you will have to choose to believe God or the devil. Your choice will determine what you are. Will you be a ...

WORRIER OR WARRIOR?

PROPAGANDA

The method he uses to undermine you, is lying propaganda. This propaganda method was used by the Japanese against the Allies in World War II.

Tokyo Rose was on all the radio wavelengths feeding the soldiers false news with continuous reports of defeat for their forces. Old home town music was played so they would get homesick, and want to go back and live in peace. The devil uses this demoralising propaganda on God's Guerrillas. He'll say to you:

"You can't do anything!"

"You won't amount to much!"

"Even though you do try you'll fail!"

"People will laugh at you!"

"Peace is better than war!"

"I've defeated you in the past — I'll do it again!"

One question we should really ask ourselves: If we are so useless and can't achieve anything, why does the devil spend so much time telling us? If he isn't worried, why doesn't he just leave us alone and allow us to fail?

No, he's terrorised alright. Any spark of warfare in you needs to be doused with the water of propaganda, telling you of your inabilities or the need to leave things as they are.

We are now going to see different ways the propaganda can affect you, but in all cases you have a choice. You can receive what the devil says and be reduced to worry, or you can believe what God says and rise up to be a Guerrilla. What do you choose ...

WORRIER or WARRIOR?

"THE OTHER CHURCHES ARE THE ENEMY" PROPAGANDA

The church is a HOLY NATION. A nation that is neither Greek nor Jew nor male nor female. We have one common origin — Jesus Christ lives in us.

Normally, if a nation goes to war, the entire country is involved in the WAR EFFORT. It brings a unity to the people and bonds them together as never before. Israel was made up of 12 tribes. They lived and operated separately. However, when the trumpet of warfare was sounded, they became one united army.

I believe that God wants to join His tribes, His denominations, together as a unified force as never before. He wants a people so unified that the unsaved will know that we are His disciples by our love and commitment to one another.

Having a common enemy and a combined war effort will help achieve this.

We have witnessed this in our Guerrilla teams we have sent overseas. People from all denominational backgrounds fighting together for a common cause. Fighting together overcomes the minute differences of our tribal backgrounds and genuine new relationships and understanding are birthed during the war.

If ever the church needed bonding together, it is NOW. What is an answer? A common war effort.

What is needed is a clear and precise picture of who the enemy really is. It is not the church down the road. It is the devil and his works over people's lives.

We have a choice. Do we WORRY about what the other churches are doing, or do we get the overall picture and become joint WARRIORS with them in seeing what the devil and his works are doing? You can choose today ...

A denominational WORRIER or a unity WARRIOR?

'PEACE — YOU'RE OK' PROPAGANDA

Even as you are completing this book, the thoughts of peace propaganda are probably already settling into your mind:

"This is not really for you."

"You're not the warfare type!"

"Life isn't all that bad the way it is."

"You're doing a pretty good job."

"Forget about it."

"Leave it to someone else."

You had better quickly examine yourself.

Where are those thoughts coming from?

Is that God speaking to you?

NO ! WAKE UP YOU MIGHTY MAN!

Friend, you may be in relative peace now, but the war is hotting up. Isaiah tells us *"... When the enemy comes in like a flood, The Spirit of the Lord will lift up a standard against him."* (Isaiah 59:19)

Obviously a flood of the devil's works is rising up at the moment and perhaps you are only being a little put out by the "trickle" of his works. But be warned, the flood won't miss anyone who can't protect himself.

Can you imagine an untrained, unarmed man being threatened by a black belt karate expert? He'd be scared stiff. That is the picture of the majority of Christians today. Unarmed and constantly threatened by the devils works.

Can you picture a fully trained soldier armed with his rifle being afraid of the noise and performance of the same black belt? No fear no concern there. He'd just smile peacefully and pull the trigger.

God wants to raise a standard. The standard of Christian he wants, is to be able to remain perfectly calm and peaceful under fire and be able to fire a few rounds off, under His direction. You need to be that strong in your God that: *"A thousand may fall at your side, and ten thousand at your right hand;, but it shall not come near you."* (Psalm 91:7)

To have that standard, to have the peace and calm and ability to defend and fight back, you need to learn to use your weapons.

He has told us the works that He did, we shall do also. He has told us that signs and wonders will follow us.

It is time to choose whether you want a future of harrassment and constant worry, or pick your weapons of warfare and begin to use them.

What do you choose ...

WORRIER OR WARRIOR?

"PRAYER" PROPAGANDA

"Oh I'll never be talked out of praying," you may say. "Whenever there is trouble, that's the first thing I do."

We do not doubt that everyone prays in the midst of turmoil. The question is, what is your MOTIVATION? Are you a PRAYER WORRIER or PRAYER WARRIOR?

A prayer WORRIER listens to all the propaganda lies and becomes terrorised and fearful. They immediatcly flee to their prayer closet and pray out of a motivation of fear. The prayer puts them in retreat and they plead with God to do something on their behalf.

Picture, if you would, inexperienced soldiers in a conventional army coming under heavy enemy artillery bombardment. They get on the radio and scream out to headquarters:

PRAYER WORRIER

OR
PRAYER WARRIOR

"Help. Get us out of here!"
"Were going to die!"
"Don't just sit there, do something!"
" Help! Help! Help! Help!"

If they just continued screaming out in fear and not listening for advice, their commanding officers could offer little assistance. Their General could be trying to get through instructions of how to counter-attack, but fear had stopped their ability to hear.

Many inexperienced Guerrillas find themselves screaming out to the Lord when they get under heavy spiritual bombardment.

We have cried out in the midst of our trouble and apparently God did not hear. When He sees that we have had teaching on the areas of authority in prayer. He expects us to act as He would act. Remember the works that Jesus did, we do also. Can you imagine Jesus screaming out to God in terror?

We are to quietly seek God's direction in the situation and then be obedient and counter-attack. If you choose not to be moved by worry propaganda, your mind will be at peace and you will see the situation clearly. The Lord may remind you of the instruction on attacking prayer aimed at binding the devil's power. Your warrior prayer will then break through.

Even in prayer, you can choose to be motivated by fear or God's word.

If you are under threat, retire to your prayer closet, calmly ask for God's power and direction so you can counter attack in prayer, and then peacefully and strongly walk out into the battle once again and do His works.

You have a choice — what will you be ...

A PRAYER WORRIER OR A PRAYER WARRIOR?

"HE'S NOT WITH YOU" — PROPAGANDA

Many of us, after prayer, deciding to believe God's word and step out, are faced with a last blast of propaganda.

In the principles of warfare listed in Deuteronomy 20, the priests were commanded to tell the troops:

"... You are on the verge of battle with your enemies; do not let your heart faint, do not be afraid, and do not tremble or be terrified because of them; for the Lord your God is He who goes with you..." (Deuteronomy 20:3-4)

The first piece of propaganda he uses is: "God is not really with you". Well the devil is sometimes half right. God is not really "with" you, that's true. But the other half of the truth is that God's Guerrillas have a better covenant than that of the old testament army. He's not "with us" but "in us". We walk out to battle but underneath our human covering there lies a "SPIRITUAL SUPERMAN" ready to work through us with His strength and power.

You are spiritual Clark Kents moving out to battle.

However if that wasn't enough for you, God also gives us extra promises of protection as we go to war:

"The angel of the Lord encamps all around those who fear Him, and delivers them." (Psalm 34:7)

One time while ministering in New Zealand in a crusade, a woman suddenly stood up and ran out of the meeting. Later, directed by the pastor, she came to us for counselling.

She had been a witch, in charge of many covens, but had seen the truth of Jesus and wanted to be set free. She apologized for running out of the meeting but told us she had been absolutely terrorized because of the semi circle of angels who were camped about me while I preached. The sight of such awesome Godly power had scared her so much, she just couldn't stay. Now, I am no different from any of God's servants, because His promise for angelic protection is for all.

Sometimes when we go out to battle, we face the propaganda machine saying "You're all alone, you're outnumbered. We are going to make mince meat out of you!" If you were Clark Kent walking down the street with King Kong on one side and Captain Marvel on the other, you would not be too concerned. Everyone would be getting out of your way.

That is how the devil and demons see it. That is how that witch saw it. A Spiritual Superman coming their way with Spiritual Body Guards. If he can't bluff you with propaganda then he knows he is defeated.

Remember you have a choice. Believe God's Word which says:

"For He shall give His angels charge over you, To keep you in all your ways." (Psalm 91:11)

You can believe the devil when he says you're alone, or you can believe God. You make the choice; which is it ...

A SUPER WORRIER OR A SUPER WARRIOR?

"YOU'RE NOT GOOD ENOUGH" — PROPAGANDA

Although "afraid" may be the correct title for a few, I believe the majority of our fears have been brought about by past failure. As we previously mentioned, failure has made us search for "other ministries." Some have said: "Well, I tried that witnessing and praying for the sick and it didn't work out for me."

After such a failure, it's easy for the devil's propaganda machine to start pumping distorted facts into your mind:

"Well, that proves it!"

"You're not good enough!"

"A real soldier would have been successful!"

"You are not Guerrilla material!"

In response, many have put their rifles and grenades in the corner and have decided to "wait on" God to see what their real ministry is. The trouble is they have been waiting and waiting and waiting.

Remember you are still in boot camp training. Can you imagine a normal soldier in boot camp going out to the practice range and scoring 10 out of 10? I'm sure most recruits don't have great results initially.

Can you imagine that new recruit sitting in the corner worrying and considering what other career he'd take on? If that master sergeant caught him, I'm sure he'd get blasted:

"Son, you're in the army and if it takes 100 years we're going to make a soldier of you. Now get out to the range with the rest and practise.

God does not want you sitting around being a worrier.

The warrior apostle Paul had the right attitude when everything wasn't going too well for him. In Philippians 3:12 he says:

"Not that I have already attained, or am already perfected, but I press on, that I may lay hold of that for which Christ Jesus has also laid hold of me."

Why did Christ lay hold of Paul? TO DO HIS WORKS!

Why did Christ lay hold of you? TO DO HIS WORKS!

Now you may not have already attained or been perfected but it does not mean you sit down in self pity and worry — you press on.

You are like everybody, and like Paul you will have set-backs, but you have a choice. A choice to look at the past failures, or to press ahead to the promise of God to make you a warrior.

Paul knew how to choose. He goes on to say:

"... Forgetting those things which are behind and reaching forward to those things which are ahead." (verse 13)

There may be some of us who have "missed it" and lost a battle or two. Remember the war is made up of many battles. You can lose a battle and still win the war. The choice is up to you. You can believe the devil if you want to.

Satan says to you the exact reverse:

"Remember those failures which are behind and don't reach for the wonderful promises of God which are ahead. It's not for you!"

OR you can be the warrior like Paul. He had the promise, the works that Jesus did shall he do also and greater works, and he reached towards that.

GOOD OLD DAYS

Let's not continue to look back to the days of Joshua and say: "Boy, if I was only around then."

Don't look back longingly at the days of Paul and Peter and say: "Gee, these guys had all the excitement."

Don't dwell worriedly when we read of Finney, Spurgeon and Smith Wigglesworth and say:

"Wow, they were the good old days."

I tell you, God's Guerrillas, we will be looking back in future years and recalling our war victories:

"Oh that crusade in India was the memorable." "Do you recollect when we took the Philippines?" "Remember when we turned our hometown around for Jesus?"

"AH yes, the 1980's and 90's, they were the good old days. The days when we turned the world upside down for Jesus."

SAINTS; THESE ARE THE GOOD OLD DAYS!

Come on, Guerrillas, your training has only just begun. Pick up these grenades, dust off your rifle, hear the trumpet call to battle.

No Longer a WORRIER BUT NOW A WARRIOR

how you can Heal the Sick

"THE BELIEVERS DO IT YOURSELF GUIDE TO DIVINE HEALING"

by
Stuart Gramenz

For a full list of books, cassettes, videos and teaching material write to:

International Outreach
P.O. Box 64
Newstead
Queensland 4006
Australia

International Outreach
P.O. Box 17 -051
Greenlane
Auckland 5
New Zealand

International Outreach
46 Tessall Lane
Longbridge
Birmingham B31 2SF
England

For a full list of Sovereign World International books write to:

Sovereign World Ltd.,
P.O. Box 17,
Chichester,
West Sussex PO20 6RY,
England

Sovereign World Ltd.,
6 Wambiri Place,
Cromer,
NSW 2099,
Australia

Sovereign World Ltd.,
P.O. Box 24-086,
Royal Oak,
Auckland,
New Zealand

Sovereign Books,
14 Balmoral Road,
Singapore 1025